THE RELIGIOUS EXPERIENCE
OF REVOLUTIONARIES

Eugene C. Bianchi

The
RELIGIOUS EXPERIENCE
of REVOLUTIONARIES

Doubleday & Company, Inc.
Garden City, New York, 1972

ACKNOWLEDGMENTS

"Year of Our Lord" and "Catechumen" from NO ONE WALKS WATERS,
copyright © 1964, 1966 by Daniel Berrigan; "Children in the Shelter"
from NIGHT FLIGHT TO HANOI, copyright © 1968 by Daniel Berrigan,
S.J.; "To the Prisoners" from FALSE GODS, REAL MEN, copyright ©
1969 by Daniel Berrigan, S.J.. Reprinted by permission of the Macmillan
Company.
Excerpts from TRIAL POEMS and THE TRIAL OF THE CATONS-
VILLE NINE by Daniel Berrigan. Reprinted by permission of Beacon
Press.
"The Making of Malcolm X" by Eugene Bianchi. Copyright © 1972 by
Eugene Bianchi. Used by courtesy of Sign Magazine (June, 1972
issue).

ISBN: 0-385-05412-2
Library of Congress Catalog Card Number 72-76122
Copyright © 1972 by Eugene C. Bianchi

For Cathryn . . . a free spirit

ACKNOWLEDGMENTS

I am particularly indebted to the graduate and undergraduate students at Emory University who helped me formulate and develop the ideas in this book. I am also grateful to Professor Jack Boozer of Emory's religion department for his critical reading of the text and to Frank R. Cetani for his helpful suggestions. I want to thank Mrs. Grayce Farmer for her patient deciphering and typing of the manuscript. Finally, I owe a special thanks to my wife, Cathryn, who supplied direct assistance in preparing the text and the indirect aid of encouragement in the "down" moments of researching and writing.

CONTENTS

THE RELIGIOUS EXPERIENCE
OF REVOLUTIONARIES

I am told that religion and politics
are different spheres of life. But I
would say without a moment's hesitation
and yet in all modesty that those who
claim this do not know what religion is.

Mahatma Gandhi

I - Guidelines for Exploring Revolutionary Religiousness

In this book, I want to explore the religious experience of six revolutionary persons. Since the religious experience concerns concrete individuals, it is not enough to relate such religiousness to abstract theories about revolution. What I will call dissenting spirituality, needs to be studied in the thought and action of particular revolutionaries as experiencing subjects. This project calls for a broad understanding of the religious experience as deeply related to what is ordinarily seen as the secular, human experience. In this first chapter, I intend to establish a flexible framework of guideline questions for investigating the religious experience in novel ways. What is it about the thinking, writing, and life style of these six figures that manifests the religious experience? Can we understand the most profound manifestations of being religious as intrinsically related to daily, secular existence? Are there universal traits of dissenting religiousness that extend beyond the usual demarcations of traditional understandings of religious experience?

I chose these six persons in part because of the availability of documentation by and about them. Four of them are dead, thus leaving a largely finished personal corpus of writings. The two living subjects are much publicized and, therefore, easy to follow through their continuing involvements. Furthermore, all the characters are Westerners, an element that restricts considerably the cultural environment of their lives. Again, these men are contemporary figures, who share the political and social dilemmas of mid-twentieth-century life. What I will call the religious experience of these men is closely linked to the experiences shared in the cultural matrix of our time.

But the most important reason for this choice of subjects was the desire to obtain a wide variety of personalities. Diversity of type is crucial for undergirding a chief thesis of my book: that a religiousness with similar traits pervades the lives of men with heterogeneous backgrounds. Diversity among revolutionaries also underscores another theme: beneath the political or the traditionally religious rhetoric of these men, a religious experience can be detected that is intrinsic to their secular experience. Flowing from this is a third and culminating thesis: the religious experience intrinsic to the secular experience itself is a most profound dimension of what it means to be religious or to "have religion."

In light of these assumptions, it became necessary to select men who found inspiration in traditional religious heritages as well as persons who rejected those institutional inheritances. For I hope to demonstrate that Christianity-rejecting Che Guevara experienced as full a sense of religiousness in his revolutionary strivings as did the black preacher Martin L. King, Jr., who openly acknowledged his debt to Protestant Christianity. Another way of stating this is to claim that the specifically religious language of Jesuit Daniel Berrigan and that of Muslim Malcolm X are symbolic code words pointing to basic experiences that reveal fundamental human religiousness.

In this approach I am not arguing, as some contemporary theologians have, that atheists are anonymous Christians or, for that matter, latent Muslims. On the contrary, I am affirming that the secular experience is not to be reduced to a traditionally religious (Christian, Muslim, Jewish) meaning or symbolization, as though the latter were the deepest and definitive meaning of being religious. The anonymous Christianity argument usually presupposes that there are religious qualities in non-Christians or humanists that can be understood as starting points on the journey to the fullness of religion. The latter is ordinarily associated with a specific religious tradition. The themes of this book are rather a challenge to the approach of "latent Christianity." Christianity or any other concrete religious heritage takes on meaning in as much as it fosters the development of a religiousness intrinsic to being human.

Most of this chapter will be devoted to describing a working model of the religious experience that will serve as a flexible filter for analyzing the subjects under investigation. In these introductory remarks, I wish to clarify general goals of the project. By delineating the intrinsic religiousness of the secular experience, I hope to contribute to a broader understanding of human religiousness. This quest is not a denial of the value of particular religious traditions as they have developed in Western history. Rather, these specific traditions are still capable of symbolizing in powerful ways man's search for meaning in face of the dilemmas of ultimacy and mystery in human life. Yet these particular heritages are varied expressions of a religious core in what most people consider to be only profane or mundane.

This study can also be seen as a quest for a more profane ecumenism. In the past decade, ecumenism has meant the renewed efforts of churches to re-establish unity in matters of doctrine, polity, and mission. This movement also fostered a spirit of dialogue with non-Christian religions. The term "secular ecumenism" was coined to describe the collaboration of churches in promoting the worldly causes of peace and justice. Although these currents have been largely laudable, they all suffer from an overly ecclesiastical emphasis. An important task remains undone, that of elaborating a kind of profane ecumenism. This involves moving beyond the confines of church unity to discover and develop a religiousness of human unity. Only when such ecumenism is viewed as presenting what is most deeply religious in all men will the various kinds of churchly superiority complexes be overcome. A new kind of foundation for human brotherhood on religious grounds will begin to be laid.

The limitations and tentativeness of this endeavor should be recognized. Not only is the study limited to a few persons, but it is also restricted to revolutionary types. The search for a more universal and intrinsic religiosity cannot be contained by the revolutionary experience alone. The latter is just one aspect of a much larger picture. Even within the radical and revolutionary culture of today, other styles of life and action might have been explored. Given these limitations, I selected dissimilar personalities to underline a conviction about creativity in religious studies. Original patterns are often disclosed only by making unusual associations or even seemingly unwarranted assertions. Most people would not look on Che Guevara, Frantz Fanon, and Abbie Hoffman as religious men. On the other hand, many would not interpret the radical, secular activity of Berrigan and King as the truly religious dimension of these persons.

Some may question the use of "revolutionary" in reference to the men studied in this volume. In a more restricted sense, a revolutionary is one who works for the complete overthrow of political structures and cultural values. Che Guevara, Malcolm X, Frantz Fanon, and perhaps Abbie Hoffman would qualify as revolutionaries in this strong sense. Yet even in this group, Malcolm X tempered his earlier radicalism by offering American society the alternative of ballots or bullets. While Hoffman's Yippie stance diametrically opposes the competitive ethos of capitalist society, he does not propose military confrontation but rather a dramatically challenging counterculture. King and Berrigan are classed as radical critics of society, but they do not call for a total reversal of national institutions and ideology. I am therefore using "revolutionary" in a looser perspective, signifying men who radically challenge the structures and mores of the prevailing culture. The revolutionary spectrum ranges from violent opposition to subtle undermining of received values and institutions.

In a final chapter, I will draw together from the concrete lives of these revolutionaries some marks of a dissenting spirituality. The present age requires a communal, worldly, dialectical style of spirituality, a mysticism or mystique of dissent. This study of revolutionaries can provide an open, realistic, and liberated way of living one's convictions, which I interpret as being religious. This, again, is not to claim that dissenting spirituality is the only mode of religious existence. Rather, it asserts that such a mystique has for too long been neglected and underdeveloped by both religionists and churches. Moreover, in this era of accelerated revolutionary consciousness, dissenting spirituality takes on special relevance.

Religiousness and Its Expression

What is meant by the religious experience in reference to contemporary revolutionaries? The work of Paul Tillich and other modern thinkers about religion as a pervasive dimension of human life can best serve as a basis for this inquiry. Religion has to do with concern for ultimate values in and through past, present, and future realities. These worldly realities are of worth in themselves and are to be embraced for themselves as long as they do not become idolatrous. Idolatry, or anti-religion, signifies worship of conditioned and relative values in a way that shuts a person off from openness to fuller enhancement of values in self, neighbor, and community, and in reference to nature. Religion, therefore, is not primarily a set of beliefs in a deity or in a code of ethics propounded by a church. Rather, religiousness consists primordially in a total attitude toward life and the world. The religious experience involves an attitude of concern or reverence toward earthly realities that is itself symbolically open to transcendent realizations of value. My interest is to see how this kind of religiousness is manifested in the concrete lives of the six subjects.

Such a study of religiousness in contemporary life would appear to meet insurmountable difficulties because of the secularized mentality of modern man. How can his worldly experiences be interpreted as religious? Modernity seems to reject any transcendent goals for human life. Yet such a conclusion would be superficial and mistaken. Abraham Maslow noted in his clinical investigations that persons who disclaim traditional theistic adherence reveal a fuller sense of religiousness in their secular experience than the more compartmentalized denominational religionists. The religious experience can be found in its deepest dimensions within the secular experience. In the life of contemporary revolutionaries, these religious experiences will assume a specific content and special nuances. But what Langdon Gilkey calls "a phenomenology of religious apprehension in secular life" remains an imperative both for a fuller understanding of human existence and also as a prolegomenon to theological discourse.

Religious symbols are not tales about exterior happenings, but, rather, imaginative modes of talking about the human condition. A living participation in these symbols tends to unify a fragmented existence and opens into creative relationships with others and the world. The criteria for adequacy or worth of these symbols is their ability to move men toward the transformation of themselves and their society in life-giving directions. Whatever destroys or impedes the growth of freedom in personal and communal life is irreligious or demonic. There is a tendency to confine religious symbols to traditional understandings of myth and ritual. This approach fails to see how extensively religious phenomena pervade all important human endeavors. In the following discussion about aspects of human experience that symbolize an openness to transcendence in revolutionaries, I will be applying the notion of religious symbols to attitudes and actions that are usually considered profane, or not religious of themselves.

I understand religion or religiousness, therefore, as the dimension of life wherein a man's most intensive and pervasive concerns become value-enhancing, concrete symbols that open him to participation in the realm of transcendent value. This view of the religious experience can be condensed into a working formula: *the experience of personal self-transcendence toward freedom in community.* For the rest of this chapter, I will discuss the symbols of this self-transcendence under the rubrics of subjective and objective. The former refer to the inner motivating images of coherence, wonder, and morality that give a sense of wholeness and satisfaction to a revolutionary's life and that open him to transcendent possibilities for becoming. The objective symbols are those master motivating images such as God or New People that act as external lures for personal and communal fulfillment. It should be stressed that the subjective and objective symbols are in fact part of one internalized human experience. But, for the sake of an orderly presentation of questions relating to the religious experience of revolutionaries, the distinction may be helpful.

The secular experience of revolutionaries manifests subjective symbols of transcendence. These can be divided into three groups for the sake of convenience, although a certain overlapping is always present: symbols of coherence, of wonder, and of morality. Coherence, wonder, and morality provide categories for studying the subjective experiences of being human. These classifications are, of course, arbitrary and not exclusive, but they form a framework for analyzing the intellectual, affective, and choice-oriented dimensions of life. The positive symbols of coherence are those drives or tendencies by which a person strives to establish a sense of order in his relations to nature and to other people. The revolutionary manifests a propensity for ordering his universe by means of an ideology. This involves an attitude toward nature, the self, and society. For example, classical Marxism projects a communal sense of coherent ordering of the world. It claims an authentic grasp of basic socioeconomic relationships that presently vitiate the healthy ordering of men and nature in capitalist countries. After the revolution, a socialist society would alter the attitudes and styles of productive activity in a co-operative rather than competitive direction. The result of these changes, in the Marxist analysis, would allow men to harmonize or properly order their alienated lives. New creative relationships to the material world as well as to human and animal creatures would be established. A number of contemporary Marxist thinkers have emphasized the unfinished and open-ended aspects of their world view in contrast to the idolatrous absolutizing of Stalinist concepts of communism.

Another example of the drive toward a better ordering of the world can be found in the unlikely case of anarchist individualists. Such visionaries of a new order fear the authoritarian perils of all bureaucratic states, even those formed by classical Marxists. Yet this anarchist abhorrence of absolute ideology linked to total bureaucratic power does not result in a rejection of order. It is, rather, a search for coherence that maximizes the fulfillment of persons within society. The change of emphasis is significant, but it does not eliminate the fashioning of a coherent world view. This revolutionary drive to coherence, as a reflective process of the human mind, reveals an openness to transcendent possibilities and therefore implies a religious experience. Only static and idolatrous ideologies reject transcendent possibilities in history and can thus be said to be irreligious. Hitler's Aryan absolutism is an example of an irreligious symbol of coherence. Rather than contribute to self-transcendence toward freedom in community, it stifled freedom and brotherhood.

I have been dealing with the reflective, or theoretical, aspects of these world views. Yet, a deeper consideration of these symbols of order would urge us to look beneath philosophical reflection to that prereflective, primary level of understanding that undergirds theoretical symbols of coherence. For the personal experience of revolutionaries manifests a fundamental trust in reality, a confidence which is the basis for formulating any world view. It can be described as a kind of human faith in order as such, a faith closely related to man's fundamental trust in reality. Thus the revolutionary's striving to overcome a situation judged oppressive and to build a better society would be meaningless if it did not stem from a prereflective sense of confidence in an order whence purpose and coherence could be fashioned. Of course, the revolutionary is not attempting to find or reconstruct an old order, as though all purposeful structures were already given in the world and need only be restored or rediscovered. He is, rather, forming a novel structure, a new style of societal interaction; he is not restoring a past coherence but creating a new one. Yet all these endeavors to bring about a new order of social interaction are predicated on a radical confidence in the trustworthiness of nature and history. At its deepest level, the symbols of coherence reveal a faith in man's abilities to redirect a purpose intrinsic to the world.

The symbols of wonder are those aspects of human experience that manifest an attitude of exaltation or celebration about the world, the self, and the human community. In all these ways, intimations of transcendence are present, so a sense of religiousness is experienced. A communication with and celebration of nature has characterized religious mystics throughout history. The beauties of nature have been portals through which religious gurus glimpsed the transcendent and led others toward fuller sensitivity to unsuspected and ineffable experiences. Most revolutionaries do not excel in showing such appreciation of nature. The political, social, and economic causes that they espouse occupy the greater part of their interest. Yet poetic and dramatic radicals such as Berrigan and Hoffman portray a reverence and relish for the beauties and pleasures of earth.

If the scope of celebration is extended to the arts of all kinds, an appreciation of such creativity can be more widely discovered. It will also be important to note how a person's ability to be religious is diminished by insensitivity toward beauty in nature and art. The celebration of beauty is often expressed in ritual acts, which are also found in revolutionary life. Special rites unify and strengthen central ideological commitments. Certain forms of humor and play are associated with revolutionary rites or involvements. The playful and humorous aspects of life are ways of transcending limitations and adversity through a kind of hopeful "wager" that evil will not prevail over good in future situations.

The symbols of coherence and of morality tend to reflect man the active molder of himself and his environment. Order and morality also presuppose a certain givenness of the world and human tradition, but they both depend strongly upon man the fabricator, the one who actively fashions unifying forms in nature and history. By contrast, the symbols of wonder emphasize passive and more emotional qualities. Aggressive, controlling intellect and will give place to responsive enjoyment and acceptance of diversity, vitality, and feeling. The latter aspect of living has often been noticed in saints and poets whose visionary religiosity pioneered future developments. The same type of visionary projection, as a transcendent movement into an unknown future, can also form a revolutionary's religiousness.

These modes of opening a person to transcendence, to dimensions beyond the immediate and the material, can be experienced individually or collectively. Thus the delight of accepting and responding to friendship and community constitutes a positive religious experience. Trusting human communication and acceptance lift a person beyond his limited selfhood and tie him again ("religion" is related to the Latin *religare:* to refasten) to transcendent potentials for living. This implies a religiousness in as much as the person is drawn beyond himself (self-transcendence) to experience more fully his real inner self, draw closer to other persons, and remain open to still-mysterious and unrealized values. Yet symbols of wonder are more difficult to describe than those of coherence and morality. While the latter can be analyzed in conceptual terms, affective experiences relating to nature, self, and community can only be pointed to after the experience. The elusiveness of these signs of transcendence does not diminish their importance. Indeed they constitute some of the most privileged moments of self-transcendence.

The symbols of wonder that pertain to human community are closely linked to symbols of morality. The positive signs of enjoyment of what is and openness to the new carry with them questions of choice, of ethical decision. The latter belong more in the realm of the intellectual and volitional than in that of the intuitive, emotional, and sensual. But the experiences of wonder cannot thrive unless they exist in an environment of justice, freedom, and peace. In his struggles for freedom and justice, the revolutionary can experience transcendence. In joining the movement of a people to overcome alienation and oppression, the revolutionary takes risks that defy and exceed merely human calculation.

The works of justice and liberation raise him above himself, give him a potential to become more than he is. The revolutionary ethic is the motivational force for establishing a kind of community that in its ideal condition tends toward the ultimate. As an ideal, such a community is transcendent in its co-operative and egalitarian aspects. The "blessed" community of the revolutionary's dreams is an unrealized and perhaps unrealizable dimension of his eschatology. Yet it is precisely this transcendent dimension that unites the ethical quest for such a community with religiousness. Other questions about revolutionary morality will also have to be asked. What are the principle virtues that he cultivates? How does he devise a criterion of conscience for making ethical choices? Is his moral sense conducive to actions that foster freedom in community?

The ethics that inspire the revolutionary manifest significant symbols of his process of self-transcendence. His inner judgments about justice and brotherhood, as well as his actions of morality, constitute key motivational factors of religiousness. The writings and actions of the men studied in this book are imbued with ethical passion for racial, class, and human rights. The issues of political oppression, racial discrimination, and military aggression are implicitly or explicitly dealt with in terms of an acute sense of morality. These volitional norms are closely tied with the revolutionary's intellectual framework (symbols of coherence) and his affective experiences of wonder. The ethical, in the broadest sense (i.e. beyond narrow moralism), defines the realm of experience through which men actively change and develop their given situation in concert with others. The ethical is the domain of decision and action toward possible achievements that, in the mind of the revolutionary, will enhance the values of individual and communal life. This enhancement implies a transcendence, a going beyond the present limitations of an oppressive situation: thus a religiousness.

The ethical dimension of the revolutionary is related to another significant element of self-transcendence, namely, suffering. As he struggles to achieve his goals, the revolutionary meets painful opposition. His moral solidarity with the poor and oppressed demands that he enter into their suffering. Moreover, his own leadership position makes it more likely that what he sees as the oppressor's retaliation will fall especially on him. The forces of injustice and destruction inflict a constant suffering on the revolutionary. Moreover, he may have to suffer because of misunderstandings and evils within the revolutionary community. Yet this suffering can be integrated as a purifying and ennobling dynamism in the revolutionary's inner development. Willingness to endure suffering and to transform pain is a touchstone of his leadership. It is also an intrinsic element of his self-transcendence toward novel realizations of value; suffering becomes a mark of his religiousness.

Since this study focuses on the religiousness of revolutionaries, it is less necessary to criticize their latent or overt morality. I want to avoid a naively uncritical approach concerning the consequences of actions, particularly in the area of violent means. But I am primarily interested in a revolutionary's morality in as much as it discloses the subjective motivational impetus toward self-transcendence. It is enough to ask general questions about a revolutionary's morality as a contributing factor to religiousness. Does it clearly lead to self-destruction of the person or to the manifest disintegration of human community? If we can be satisfied on these counts, we can bracket off the more refined issues involved in comparing a revolutionary's ethic to other styles of morality.

Closely associated with ethical impulses in a revolutionary's life are the dilemmas stemming from the existential predicament of being human. The existential pertains to personal experiences of inner ambiguity about the human situation; it concerns chiefly man's fundamental position as a value-laden but limited and death-prone entity. The existential, as I am using it, refers to decisions that are made about those features of existence such as mortality, temporality, and contingency. These experiences flow from the ineluctable "givenness" of the finite predicament. In the ethical domain, the subject can decide in ways that alter an individual or communal situation. In the existential area, a person faces what is impossible to change.

But he must take some judgmental stand, if it be only the stand of ignoring his fate, in face of these existential absolutes. Yet, in both the ethical realm of coping with potentialities for personal and communal growth and in the existential domain of dealing with the immutable ambiguities of a finite freedom, religious experiences emerge. For, just as the sufferings linked with the ethical can dispose a person to greater depth and maturity, so, too, the pain of the existential situation can lead to a heightened self-awareness and a transcending integration of life purpose. It is not only the negative dimension (suffering) of the ethical and existential that can provide subjective motivation for self-transcendence. The positive aspects of ethical strivings and the positive accommodations to existential inevitabilities become means of self-transcendence toward more excellent modes of being.

Participation in the objective and subjective symbols of self-transcendence forms a continuous process in human life. It would certainly exemplify Whitehead's fallacy of misplaced concreteness were we to credit each of the above categories with a discrete and atomically identifiable existence. Although these distinctions may provide some order for reflection on the religious experience of revolutionaries, self-transcendent religiousness must be viewed as a process at once organic and dynamic. This process is not usually at the threshold of explicit consciousness in any person; moreover, the process of self-transcendence is not an uninterrupted climb to ever higher levels of living. The dynamism of self-transcendence is best described, therefore, as a continuous *metanoia*, a change of mind and heart experiences that includes retrogression and advancement, moments of darkness and of light, of suffering and of exaltation.

This ongoing conversion, or *metanoia*, is akin to the Christian symbolism of death/resurrection and to the Hebrew imagery of Exodus, that is, the movement from enslavement to freedom. In keeping with an underlying theme of this study, I would affirm that such familiar imagery of *metanoia* in traditional religions constitutes significant code language for a process at work in all men. All finite freedoms questing for self and communal fulfillment undergo these conversion experiences to a more or less intense degree in the encounters of living. The painful dimensions of this *metanoia* are located in an acceptance of finitude and in the unmasking of personal and collective idolatries. The negative aspect, the dark and suffering side, of the religious *metanoia* disposes and opens a person to the experience of novel, transcendent possibilities. Thus the religious experience, with its specific nuances in revolutionary figures, is to be understood in a holistic and dynamic sense as the *metanoia* of life itself perceived in its deepest dimensions.

The subjective aspects of the religious experience would remain incomplete and inadequate, however, were I to rest content with the following summation: the experience of personal self-transcendence viewed as a continuing *metanoia*. Two more elements need to be added to the understanding of religiousness. The first consists in a clearer grasp of the proximate and remote goals of the religious dynamism in man; I call this aspect "freedom." Secondly, it is essential to explore more explicitly the context of human religiousness; I will attempt this under the rubric of "community."

The movement of self-transcendence is toward greater freedom in personal and communal life. In general, freedom is understood as the domain of transcendent possibilities for man. Through growth in freedom, he is able to exercise more fully his potentialities and to enhance self and societal values. The development of the potential of his manhood implies more than an unfolding of a determined "given" in man, although, of course, limitations in individuals and communities act as curtailments of material and spiritual achievement. Yet I want to underscore the newness, or originality, of the experiences of freedom. For example, the newly realized revolutionary consciousness as a freeing experience is not merely the expression of a past datum in the revolutionary's personality. It is a uniquely new state of mind for him with broad ramifications for consciousness and conduct. The same novelty can be ascribed to a community's gradual realization of freedom, when a more co-operative and egalitarian attitude is embraced.

How a person copes with the contingencies and necessities related to freedom will also bear on the quality of his religiousness. The question can be put: how free is the revolutionary? In the realm of the contingent, he is free to foster a wide spectrum of personal and communal values. Yet the means that he employs in promoting these values may be destructive for his own long-term growth in freedom. Rapid, surface achievements of freedom through the exercise of brutal means can so debase the inner person as to make authentic advancement in self-transcendence virtually impossible. The implications of this stunting of freedom can be best discussed in terms of community. But even on an individual level, personal motivations of self-aggrandizement by the accumulation of power can vitiate what appears as newly attained freedom.

Moreover, the question of "how free" also relates to the realm of necessity. Physical and mental disabilities as well as the determination of mortality itself place unsurpassable confines on human freedom. A revolutionary's attitudes toward his bodily infirmities, character deficiencies, and toward death itself will reveal the quality of his freedom experiences as goals of self-transcendence. To a considerable extent, the communal projects of the revolutionary will also come under the dimension of the necessarily determined and the finitely unsurpassable. The prophet in matters of race or war, for instance, must surely recognize the probably unsurpassable limits of freedom that can be realized in the society around him. For it has been so thoroughly conditioned on a material and psychic plane in the ways of racial discrimination and of warlike diplomacy that freedom from such an inheritance can only be partial in terms of the revolutionary's lifetime. How he contends with these limitations of freedom will also impinge on the worth of his religiousness.

If freedom is understood as both the multiplication of alternatives and the qualitative richness of any particular option, a further question can be asked: where is this freedom to be exercised? Is it to be experienced within history or beyond history? It can be rightly assumed that most revolutionaries are concerned with the expansion of freedom within history. Even the freedom concerns of radical types with institutionally religious commitments are primarily centered on this-worldly liberation for oppressed individuals and groups. But it is less frequently seen that professedly secular revolutionaries do not totally limit freedom to the historical.

The luring symbol of the new humanity or of the co-operative community resides in a true sense beyond the present realizations of history. The revolutionary cannot fully understand or experience the kind of freedom intimated in these futuristic concepts. In a real sense they stand open-endedly beyond history. They connote a mysterious power in the universe to achieve a kind of freedom not yet known. Even in some future age no revolutionary would ever say that the new humanity had been completely realized; by their very nature, as humanly unrealizable concepts, such ideas point to a faith in a transcendent power to attain certain perfections of freedom that far exceed the Promethean strivings of any revolutionary community. Thus it may be possible to conclude that all the figures studied in this book would locate the realm of freedom both within and beyond history.

Is revolutionary freedom a liberation from aspects of history or from history itself? It is evident that the revolutionary presses for freedom from what are interpreted as dehumanizing oppressions imposed by economic, political, and cultural relationships. Yet the revolutionary's endeavors are also a struggle to be free from history. Is it not possible to argue that the very open-endedness of the great motivational images in revolutionary consciousness implies a sense of or a desire for release from any historically realizable configuration? Revolutionary freedom from oppression implicitly involves a stance before unconditioned and historically unrealizable possibilities. Thus even this negative dimension of freedom points to transcendent realms, that is, to a kind of co-operative society that, given the broken condition of man, will never be perfectly achieved.

The freedom of the revolutionary is also a positive freedom for new relationships between men and for new political and economic forms. It is essential in my view of the religious experience that the notion of self-transcendence be closely linked to its goal: the freedom or liberation of persons to maximize their selfhood through social intercourse. The melding of freedom experiences with religious experiences has a long history in traditional Western religious thought. The central Hebrew experience of Exodus is surrounded with historical imagery concerning human liberation from bondage. So, too, the freedom theme of the Christian scriptures, with its own set of special nuances, has been emphasized by many biblical and theological scholars. Bonhoeffer's formulation of this experience of freedom as a this-worldly transcendence is perhaps nearest to the topic that I am pursuing. I want to draw attention to how this religious, positive experience of freedom is orchestrated in the lives of revolutionary figures.

The experience of self-transcendence toward freedom as a religious phenomenon must be placed, finally, within the context of community. That the religious experience involves community, needs little argument; it is more important to investigate the basis of community for the subjects of this study. The causal factors that incline men to form community are plural. The experience of common oppression that is identified as the imposition of a particular class, race, or leader can drive persons to establish a community of goals and actions. In general, the formation of community from the experience of economic, political, or racial misery is much in evidence among revolutionaries. The latter can rise up out of such communities of misery, like Malcolm X, or they can link themselves to these movements, like Frantz Fanon, after spending a good portion of their lives as beneficiaries of the dominant culture.

The basis for a revolutionary's community is also a positive sense of specific goals to achieve and of an overriding ideal vision. In both areas his experience of self-transcendence stems from a relationship to community. The proximate goals may be the radical reform of institutions in directions of greater justice and equality for the whole community that he represents. Or his motivating vision may be some ideal realization of human community, a vision symbolized by the language of "New People" or "New Humanity." Whatever aspect of the basis for the revolutionary's community is studied, it is clear that his religious experience is a self-transcendence within a network of communal relationships.

The communal dimension of the revolutionary's religious experience involves the question of the extent and limits of freedom among freedoms. His community experience makes possible a fuller enhancement of his freedom. He is able to grow in creative dialogue and sharing participation with his fellows. In this way, a person manifests the active aspect of being a finite freedom in community. Yet community limits the revolutionary's freedom of self-assertion, because he is in contact with other persons, whose rights he should acknowledge and cede. On this point, a special problem arises for the handling of deviants in a revolutionary community.

This is not meant to imply a contradiction for individual freedom in the face of communal restrictions; on the contrary, the interplay between man's active freedom and his passive respect for the freedoms of others forms the dialectic process of his self-transcendence. Rather, a person's potentials and limitations in being a finite freedom among freedoms in community underscore a vital dimension of the religious experience. This communal factor also provides the interactive situation in which ethical judgments about the constructiveness or destructiveness of a revolutionary's ideas, decisions, and conduct can be made.

Up to this point, we have focused on the subjective symbols of self-transcendence that contribute to freedom in community. I would like to turn now to a brief consideration of the objective symbols of self-transcendence, those master images that function for the revolutionary as dynamic concepts for ultimacy, or what Tillich called the unconditioned. The unconditioned, or ultimate, the realm of deity, appears under a positive and a negative guise. In a positive light, the ultimate has traditionally been seen as source of power for all reality and especially for human life. As source it is both the ground for all that is and a gift, a gratuitous given that precedes human existence and awareness. All three major Western religious traditions profess a deity that is source as creative ground and free gift. Jewish, Muslim, and Christian doctrines of creation and of redemptive grace testify to such traits of ultimacy. Although the nature of the transcendent and its modes of nearness and distance from the world have been variously interpreted in these traditions, it has unquestionably been understood as source of power or dynamism. Moreover, the transcendent source of power in the West has been viewed as a person or at least as possessing personal characteristics.

For many revolutionaries the transcendent source of power resides in the people. This ultimate is not called "God," but it contains as source of values the sense of ground and gift. As ground of existence, nature and humanity are the surpassing wellsprings of value. They are, in a true sense, freely given gifts to every man. To envision ultimacy in the people (as nature and humanity) is not to idolize the world. It would only be idolatry if "the people" were understood as a literally finished category rather than as an *open-ended symbol* tending toward transcendent wholeness. What more can be said about the symbol "God" itself than the indefinable source of wholeness indirectly sensed in finite strivings? The frequent use of the word "God" as a literally finished, definable entity has been a chief cause of the contemporary rejection of religion.

The power or dynamism of the ultimate has appeared in dominant or irresistible ways as well as in persuasive and attractive modes. Both forms of power in the ultimate can be found in any great religion, but the dominative style was more typical of primitive and pagan religions than of the Hebrew-Muslim-Christian heritage. I hasten to add, however, that dominative power was also strongly expressed by Yahweh, Allah, and the Christ Pantocrator images in the scriptures and customs of the West. The ultimate's power has also been portrayed as the attraction of friendly persuasion and suffering solidarity. This dual focus of the power of the ultimate echoes Otto's classic distinction of transcendent power as awesome and fascinating. The former quality pertains to the negative dimensions of ultimacy, while the latter reflects the positive aspects. In a revolutionary perspective, transcendent power rests in the people, especially in its democratic and ennobling capacities. The power of the people, which transcends individuals, also gives each person a locus for participation in decision making. This in turn enhances the growth of individuals in personhood. Solidarity with the people's suffering elevates and sustains the revolutionary's suffering. Such social pain of the revolutionary struggle transcends the atomistic gestures of individuals.

Ultimacy also implies a center of transcendent worth for human history. Through defining man in relation to God, religions have traditionally ascribed worth to mankind. From a

positive point of view, the ultimate confers value by its immanent presence in all human events. This immanent presence
of ultimacy in its value-conferring role on existing realities is
only indirectly experienced. That is, the values of nature and
history, by their own partial fulfillment, point to a transcendent
need for a not-yet-achieved unity on personal, social, and cosmic
levels. Thus the ultimate as a center of value establishes a
dialectic of immanent and transcendent worth. The ultimate is
present in every finite value and yet it is also the catalyst for
transformation or higher integration of value. The ultimate embodies value in the effective, practical realm of existence, while
it also lures man and the world toward further attainment of
value.

The positive aspect of ultimacy, in sum, consists in a "yes but
more." It is a call not just to find meaning but to create fuller
meaning. The task of the revolutionary is the creation of new
worth and meaning in the struggle of responding to the people's
needs of liberation. The wish of freeing people from physical
and mental oppression becomes the fountainhead for the revolutionary's self-worth and for that of the radical community. But
liberation of the people as a value-generating aspect of ultimacy
connotes both an affirmation and a summons, a present satisfaction and a call to foster fuller value enhancements. For it is
not enough to free the people from present tyrannies; the revolutionary must also ask himself why he fights to liberate himself
and others. Is this goal simply to allow the oppressed to enjoy
the material advantages of the ruling classes with the attendant
risk of forming a more extensive class of property-coveting oppressors? Or is the revolutionary's aim to stimulate a new life
style and self-consciousness beyond the mere distribution of
goods? His purpose is to bring about a new mentality in individuals and to establish more trusting/sharing relationships in
society. Thus the liberation of the people as an ultimate focal
point of value implies the dialectic of a Yes to the immediate
goals of the revolution coupled with a No to resting satisfied
with these goals. For the people's true liberation necessitates the

further and never fully attained achievement of fashioning a new self-consciousness and life style on a personal and communal basis.

Historical religions have also been conscious of the negative dimensions of the ultimate. The realm of ultimacy has always been shrouded in mystery and ambiguity. It is not that the gods are capricious, as was supposed in classical Greece, but rather that deity, for all its likeness to and relationship with nature and history, remains nonetheless unlike and mysteriously distinct from the world. The Hebrew author wondered at the inscrutable ways of Yahweh. The negative theology of the early-medieval theologians, and the mystical tradition generally, proclaimed the discontinuity between God and the world. Kierkegaard insisted on an infinite qualitative distinction between God and man. Otto referred to the awesome and forbidding aspects of deity, and Barth stressed the otherness of God. Such often-repeated instances manifest the negative dimensions of the ultimate. The deity cannot be taken for granted, fully understood, or manipulated.

Unlikeness as a negative aspect of ultimacy can also be understood from the revolutionary's standpoint. For the transcendent purpose of liberating the people cannot be equated with material distribution and quantitative satisfaction. Moreover, the fuller revolutionary goals of creating a new self-definition of human consciousness and of its relationship to others is also a changing and elusive pursuit. It can never be adequately described or circumscribed by any revolutionary theory. To appreciate the deficiency of all political ideology is the beginning of political wisdom. Ideology as a tentative blueprint, a changeable guide for particular actions, is to some extent a revolutionary necessity. But when the revolutionary ceases to have such a limited ideology and becomes identified with his ideology in an absolutist way, he becomes in fact a counterrevolutionary. His dogmatic intransigence fixes the future of the people in the narrow confines of his faulty vision. He is in effect saying that the ultimacy of the people's liberation is not a dynamic reality always capable of creating new values. The absolutist ideologue, whatever his revolutionary pedigree, defies the ultimacy of the people by foreclosing the possibilities of history.

A second negative quality of the transcendent, closely related to its unlikeness, or otherness, is that of paradoxical judgment on individual and collective actions. Religious institutions and officials profess to be mediators of the sacred. Yet these professional advocates of ultimacy are themselves subjected to prophetic criticism for a betrayal of authentic ultimacy. The prophet declares the paradoxical No against the hypocrisy and complicity with evil of conventional and legitimate religious institutions. All religions contain only partial and fragmentary glimpses into the mysterious domain of the sacred or the transcendent.

Moreover, these institutions are conditioned by national self-righteousness, needs for security, and many other subtle cultural pressures that incline a particular religion to identify the ultimate and unconditioned with a given set of cultural relations. Evil exploits and attitudes of the society are defended or ignored by established religions. All major religious traditions of a society tend toward idolatry, i.e., the worship of their culturally conditioned version of ultimacy. They all are accomplices in more or less silent ways in the domestic and foreign wrongs perpetrated by individuals, groups, and nation-states. Against this idol worship and complicity in evil, the prophet brings the judgment and challenge of ultimacy. In the history of religions, the prophet voice for ultimacy can be spoken by an individual or a group. Moreover, prophetic criticism is not restricted to persons or movements within a particular religious tradition.

The revolutionary's thought and action are a prophetic expression of the demands of ultimacy as reflected in the unrealized welfare of the people. The oppressed state of the people, individually and socially, physically and spiritually, stands as a critical judgment on the institutions and mentality of the dominant society. The ethos of the ruling establishment is equated by its leaders with the ultimate welfare of the people. This identification constitutes the political idolatry that cloaks the establishment's perpetration of or complicity in evil. Moreover, the idolatrous equation of the ruling-class ideology with the future welfare of the people tends to suppress the desire for revolutionary consciousness in the present. The masses are contained by force or co-opted by the enticements of material goods, emotional diversions, and false categories of prestige.

Against this idolatry and consequent distortion and alienation of the popular consciousness, the revolutionary pits his message and activity. His passion for justice and freedom expresses and concretizes the transcendent vision of a more integrated and reconciled humanity. Yet, like the classic religious prophet, the true revolutionary must not allow himself to embrace the new idolatry of a hero cult. He cannot permit himself to fall into self-glorifying fanaticism by confusing the critical message of ultimacy with personal aggrandizement. Nor should he fancy his own prophetic critique to be identical with the ultimate welfare of the people. The representative of critical revolutionary ultimacy betrays the very transcendent and judgmental aspect of the desired future humanity if he identifies it with the ideology or the ethics of the present movement or leader. Moreover, the transcendent dimension of the more just and trusting humanity-to-come provides a means for flexibility in the style of his revolutionary criticism. He knows that the challenge of revolutionary theory and practice will differ from place to place.

The foregoing guidelines for examining the religious experience rest on certain presuppositions about man and his world. Man is understood as a finite freedom; an intellectual, affectional, and volitional being; an unfinished entity in quest for self-transcendence in community. The world of man displays an interpenetration of secular and sacred, of culture and religion, of immanence and transcendence. There are no special spheres for these different aspects of human existence, as if we could neatly divide the secular experience from the religious experience. The latter is a dynamic process inscribed in the very stuff of ordinary life; *the religious experience is the secular experience of self-transcendence toward freedom in community.*

Such an understanding of the religious experience will probably be seen by some as too comprehensive and not sufficiently distinguished from simply being human. They would call for limiting the proper scope of religiousness to specific historical traditions or at least to special realms of mystery distinct from profane existence. I would argue, however, that the all-pervasive view of religiousness gives it a clearer distinctiveness than either of the above positions. For it allows the religious experience to be appreciated in a holistic and integrating way. Thus the religious experience consists in the total orientation of a person—his inner life and his stance toward others and the world. Moreover, the person is also perceived in and through his secular existence as open to transcendent and uncharted possibilities. This totalizing conception of the religious experience through subjective and objective symbols of self-transcendence distinguishes it from the necessarily more restricted views of humanness in other arts and sciences.

In the chapters that follow I will attempt to explore these views of the religious experience in the life and thought of significant revolutionary personalities. I want to avoid, however, any slavish application of the above points to concrete figures. This would not only be tedious and ultimately unproductive; it would also risk serious distortion in presenting the unique revolutionary individuals as examples to prove the guidelines. I intend to operate in precisely the opposite mode. The plan of investigation is to concentrate as inductively as possible on the actual life involvements and written works of the subjects. The theoretical model of religious experience should serve as an ancillary, interpretative instrument from which to suggest meaning and direction amid a welter of discrete observations. One revolutionary will manifest a particular facet of the model more than another. Furthermore, it is important to respect the motivational symbols of the men themselves without rigidly imposing the language of this chapter on each figure. In brief, the model for investigation provides an understanding of and perspective on the religious experience. It operates as a guiding device for asking significant questions.

Bibliography

The following authors were especially helpful in formulating the guidelines for exploring the religious experience in conjunction with a phenomenological method of studying the individual revolutionaries.

Bellah, Robert N. *Beyond Belief*. New York: Harper & Row, 1970.

Berger, Peter L. *A Rumor of Angels*. New York: Doubleday & Co., 1969.

Bettis, Joseph D. (ed.). *Phenomenology of Religion*. New York: Harper & Row, 1969.

Fingarette, Herbert. *The Self in Transformation*. New York: Harper & Row, 1963.

Fontinell, Eugene. *Toward a Reconstruction of Religion*. New York: Doubleday & Co., 1970.

Freire, Paulo. *Pedagogy of the Oppressed*. New York: Herder & Herder, 1971.

Gilkey, Langdon. *Naming the Whirlwind: The Renewal of God Language*. Indianapolis: The Bobbs-Merrill Co., 1969.

James, William. *The Varieties of Religious Experience*. New York: New American Library, 1958.

Keen, Sam. *Apology for Wonder*. New York: Harper & Row, 1969.

King, Winston L. *Introduction to Religion: A Phenomenological Approach*. New York: Harper & Row, 1968.

Kristensen, W. Brede. *The Meaning of Religion*. The Hague: Martinus Nijhoff, 1960.

Langer, Suzanne K. *Philosophy in a New Key*. Cambridge: Harvard University Press, 1942.

Lonergan, Bernard. *Insight: A Study of Human Understanding*. New York: Philosophical Library, 1957.

Maslow, Abraham. *Religions, Values and Peak Experiences*. New York: The Viking Press, 1970.

Novak, Michael. *The Experience of Nothingness*. New York: Harper & Row, 1970.

O'Dea, Thomas F. *The Sociology of Religion*. Englewood Cliffs, N.J.: Prentice-Hall, 1966.

Ogden, Schubert M. *The Reality of God*. New York: Harper & Row, 1963.

Otto, Rudolph. *The Idea of the Holy.* Oxford: Oxford University Press, 1958.

Rahner, Karl. *Nature and Grace.* New York: Sheed & Ward, 1964.

Richardson, Herbert W. and Cutler, Donald R. (eds.). *Transcendence.* Boston: Beacon Press, 1969.

Ruether, Rosemary R. *The Radical Kingdom: The Western Experience of Messianic Hope.* New York: Harper & Row, 1970.

Streng, Frederick J. *Understanding Religious Man.* Belmont, Calif.: Dickenson Publishing Co., 1969.

Tillich, Paul. *What Is Religion?* Ed. by James L. Adams. New York: Harper & Row, 1969.

van der Leeuw, G. *Religion in Essence and Manifestation.* Vol. II. New York: Harper & Row, 1963.

Whitehead, Alfred N. *Religion in the Making.* Cleveland: World Publishing Co., 1960.

II - Ernesto "Che" Guevara

The purpose of this chapter is not to make out of "El Che" a saint in keeping with traditional ecclesiastical models of holy men. Nor am I trying to refashion the guerrilla hero of Cuba into an "anonymous Christian." Contemporary attempts to rationalize professed atheists into Christians tend to neglect the chosen stance of the person involved, and these efforts also betray a subtle movement to bolster fading church institutions. Without covering over the defects and even the cruelties of Guevara, my purpose will be to examine the life and work of this revolutionary personality in the light of the model of religiousness described in the previous chapter. How can we understand Che Guevara's personal experience of self-transcendence toward greater freedom in community? In interpreting the motivating images of his life, can we decipher open-ended symbols of self-transcendence that denote a religiousness intrinsic to his human existence?

Before initiating an abstract portrayal of Che's religious experience, it is important to sketch his personality traits as manifested in his brief and celebrated career. For we must not lose sight of the fact that this subject is a concrete person who was immersed in a particular Latin American context. This historical milieu is crucial for appreciating the formative elements in his human and religious genesis. He was born to a middle-class Argentinian family of modest means. He grew up in a hectic household that was open to a broad stream of relatives and friends with whom the energetic and intense youngster gained a wide experiential knowledge of people. Despite his asthmatic condition, he displayed a sense of leadership through a bold willingness to take risks and try new adventures. From his earliest years, Ernesto Guevara showed a marked indifference to material possessions, a quality that stands out in his later life. He also absorbed from his father a feeling of the viciousness of business competition, distrust for political institutions, and a keen sense of the corruptibility of the church.

His close contact with physical infirmity through his own asthma and his mother's cancer may have been decisive factors in orienting him toward medicine as a profession. But Guevara, an adventurer at heart, grew restless with the lot of an incipient doctor with prospects of bourgeois security. He traveled extensively by motor bike to explore the variegated world of South America. A significant experience in these early travels was the time spent serving at a leper colony in Peru. The desire to relieve the suffering of the unfortunate and oppressed was to become a keynote in Che's revolutionary exploits.

His revolutionary consciousness grew as he continued to witness the downtrodden situation of great masses of Latin Americans. A major turning point in his commitment to the revolutionary struggle took place during the overthrow of the Guatemalan regime in 1954. His outrage at the poverty, disease, and hunger of the people was further exacerbated by the American CIA's role in putting down that country's leftist, progressive government. The Guatemala experience was a watershed in the life of the revolutionary doctor. He became convinced that nothing short of a fundamental revolution and reorganization of social and political institutions could effect a humane society in

Latin America. He held that to work within the given systems for reform would only strengthen the domination of domestic and especially foreign exploiters.[1]

In 1955 Che met Fidel Castro and his Cuban band in Mexico City. The story of the near-catastrophic landing in Cuba in 1956 and the subsequent episodes of conquest are well known. Guevara the wandering doctor had become the revolutionary major. After his stints as a director of industry, agriculture, and banking, Che was off again in search of revolutionary adventure. He worked for a time with the Congolese rebels, then returned to Cuba before his last foray into the Bolivian mountains. His death at the hands of the Bolivian Army marked the end of Che the *guerrillero* and the beginning of the legendary and epic Che as a symbol for many radical revolutionaries.

Although Che has become a messianic figure in some circles, I am chiefly interested in the man Guevara. That personality was a complex mixture of moral and ascetic leader, of an idealist committed to win or die. His revolutionary rhetoric was uncompromising, at times inspiring, and usually well-informed. For an intense activist, he has left a considerable literary heritage. Yet this purist believed mainly in teaching by doing. He was capable of unflinching detachment from loved ones for the revolutionary cause; yet his letters to Fidel and to his family demonstrate the "sentiments of love" which he thought should characterize the true revolutionary. His spirit was that of an adventurous experimenter who had an intense dislike for sham and hypocrisy. Self-discipline and utopian vision impelled his revolutionary ventures; he even referred to his exploits as a scaling of Mount Everest.

But this Gemini personality also manifested an authoritarian and inflexible side. He could be ruthless with enemies, even when their guilt was not fully proven. But he repeatedly urged his followers to build a society in which the rights of all were protected in ways that were more humane than had been the lot of most Cubans before the revolution. His inflexible confidence in his own judgment resulted in a certain arrogance toward those who differed with him; ultimately, this passionate self-confidence led him into the fatal miscalculations of the Bolivian mountains. As one works through the documentation by and about Che Guevara, a complicated image unfolds of a latter-day revolutionary intellectual of unpredictable moods and vivid insights.

I will begin this investigation of Guevara's religiousness by examining the symbols of coherence that formed a pattern for his own experiences of self-transcendence. The scheme of meaning that led him to new heights of personal realization can be cryptically described in his own words as "redeeming humanity." This liberation of individuals and communities consisted in freedom from a state of exploited alienation for the purpose of achieving a community of persons reconciled with neighbor, state, and with their inner selves. He held that there is only one valid definition of socialism—the abolition of exploitation of man by man: ". . . the ultimate and most important revolutionary aspiration: to see man freed from alienation."[2]

For Guevara the path from alienation to reconciliation led through the zone of armed revolution. An important vanguard of the oppressed people had begun to liberate itself from its alienated past. While the vast majority still lived in that alienated condition, revolutionaries like Che were creating a new present. Thus the broadest perspective of Che consisted in making the revolution to overcome alienation (past and present) for the sake of a reconciled future. In a classically Marxist perspective, Che believed that once the chains of alienation (that is, man dominated by commodity relationships) are broken, man will reach total consciousness of his social function. But the redeeming process for history, and nature through human history, rested on the success of the revolution.

For Che, the revolution as a locus of coherent vision and motivating meaning had physical, sociopolitical, and spiritual dimensions. On the material plane, he repeatedly stated: "Our primary aim is to give a better standard of living to everyone."[3] Agrarian reform became a major focus in lands where the

wealthy few owned the means of production. He reserved a
special animus for the United States, which he saw as the
principal foreign exploiter of the hunger of the people. The
physical dimensions of the revolution called for armed struggle
in which a people's army could, in the right circumstances, overcome a professional force. He believed also that a popular in-
surrection could create the conditions for the concrete revolution,
and he saw the countryside, not the city, as the germinating
locus of revolution in Latin America. But, just as the revolution
called for military exertions, so, too, the period after the military
victory demanded sustained discipline and unselfish labor to
build the new society.

But the physical aspects of the revolution, from those of
armed battle to agrarian and industrial reconstruction, were
subordinate for Che to the sociopolitical dimensions. His sense
of the purpose of the revolution was eminently populist and
egalitarian. He urged socialist youth cadres and university students to relate to and learn from the common people. The
guerrilla groups were to see themselves not as superior persons
but as the "people in uniform"[4] and as the vanguard of the
people. Attitudes toward the ordinary people ought not be dictated by condescending charity but by humble solidarity.
Guevara was acutely desirous of crossing over from the bourgeois
life style of his early years to a new mode of leadership of the
peasant populations by thorough assimilation to their consciousness. He knew that he could not liberate the oppressor spirit in
himself or liberate the interior sense of oppression in the masses
unless he could communicate, learn, and grow with them as
equal persons. His success in this endeavor is measured to some
degree by how completely the colloquialism "che," meaning
"buddy" or "soul brother," became an accepted part of his
name.

It was essential that the people find new modes of participation
in political functions. From Che's egalitarian hopes for a single-
salary system to his frequent advocacy of political self-determination for the weak, he revealed a deep populist mystique:

". . . contact with the people—with the ideals and purity of the people—infuses in us renewed revolutionary fervor,"[5] and again, ". . . that great source of wisdom that is the people."[6] (It may be well to mention at this point that I am bracketing judgments about how well Cuba has achieved a widely participational democracy and how well the liberties of controversial Cuban intellectuals are protected.) The whole purpose of the party was to educate the people and to turn technology to serve the people. He maintained that the "vanguard revolutionary must idealize this love of the people, the most sacred cause, and make it one and indivisible."[7]

Yet, the same Guevara who could speak so eloquently about the virtues of the people could also act callously and vindictively toward people. Like other visionaries, Che was known to put down those who stood in his way. He would lash out at those who disagreed with him, although he could also be self-critical. His harshness and even cruelty seem well attested. It is more difficult to assess the sincerity of his rhetoric. Was he truly dedicated to the people's welfare or was he a self-glorifying actor "who chose to perform on the stage of reality rather than inside a theatre"?[8] The mixture of egoism and altruism in the life of any man is hard to judge. Headstrong, charismatic leaders such as Che, with gifts of eloquence and personal flair, would understandably be carried away by their own rhetoric or use it as a tool to achieve certain ends. On the whole, however, Guevara's life of risk and commitment gives weighty credence to his altruistic words about dedication to the betterment of people.

Che's coherent vision of the revolution reveals a third dimension, which pervaded and elevated the material and social aspects. The revolution was to do more than bring material advantages to all the people. It aimed at creating a new man with a new socialist consciousness. This element especially underscores the transcendent focus of Che's coherent view of revolution. On the material level, the revolution by economic and other reforms would place the people in an environment where spiritual or mental transcendence to a new consciousness would be made possible.

A key to understanding this important facet of Che's self-transcendence was his attitude about material incentives for work. Although he realized that these incentives would be necessary during the period of transition and scarcity in Cuban society, he claimed that "material incentives will not play a part in the new society being created; they will die out as we advance."[9] He believed that as the revolution progressed, material incentives joined to a spirit of alienating competition, so typical of capitalist society, would be subordinated to the development of a new co-operative and fraternal consciousness. With characteristic zeal, he tried to implant moral motivation for work throughout Cuba, only to have his fervor tempered by the realistic Castro.

Che himself fell short of this new consciousness about material possessions; his own worldly desires at times betrayed his aspirations. Moreover, he was forced to restore more material incentives for the sake of efficiency and productivity during his term as chief economic administrator. Yet, despite these failings and accommodations, he insisted: ". . . unless you create a new man, unless you change attitudes, it all ends up in greed, lust and ambition."[10] The Cuban experiment with volunteer labor exemplifies an attempt to change the consciousness of the people toward work. This volunteer labor has been criticized as a subtler form of gaining moral recognition, acclaim, and possible advancement in party circles. But the new consciousness for each person and for society at large is such a persuasive factor in Guevara's outlook as to constitute the touchstone in his vision of the revolution. It is a spiritual transcendence that forms an essential part of his religious experience.

Up to this point I have discussed the symbols of intellectual coherence that form for Che Guevara motivating elements toward personal self-transcendence. The lived revolution, therefore, becomes not only the place for the "education of honorable men,"[11] it is also the milieu for physical, social, and spiritual transcendence. When internalized, the revolution fosters the religious experience of continually passing from various alienations to new experiences of reconciliation. But beneath this coherent set of motivating symbols, there lies a prereflective area of trusting faith. This confidence in certain aspects of reality is not religious faith in the traditional sense of adherence to particular beliefs about an explicit deity. Rather, it is a basic humanistic trust in people and the world that lies at the root of all secondary reflective ideologies, whether they are explicitly God oriented or humanistically directed. But, in both cases, the prereflective trust constitutes a primal openness to and confidence in the world that precedes rationalization and ideology. This primal trusting openness is a kind of basic faith from which all experiences of self-transcendence must be built.

The life of Che Guevara manifests a number of examples of this prereflective-faith commitment that precedes and upholds his ideology. Such faith offers neither proof nor vindication for his political theory. Yet an overriding trust in people and their potential for revolutionary change marks the celebrated years of his life. His optimism concerning the formation of a co-operative socialist society was founded on a faith in the perfectibility of human conscience. Castro emphasized Che's boundless faith in the conscience of man. Che's theories about the creation of a new man and a new consciousness in society rest on a prior faith in the people to respond to the revolutionary call. It was in part an excess of this primordial confidence in the downtrodden masses that led to his betrayal and capture in Bolivia. This kind of trust, however, implies a faith leap that moves beyond the people, either as an abstraction or as concrete individuals, to involve a confidence in what can be called the mysterious benevolence of reality. Of course, Che was vividly conscious of the weight of evil in human affairs. But the point to be made here is that his trusting, pre-reflective faith in his fellow man was by its very nature a dynamic openness to the wider mystery of human and cosmic life. This primordial confidence, therefore, participates in a broader religious experience that in turn informs the concrete manifestations of the human faith leap.

It is particularly difficult to pinpoint the symbols of wonder, those moments of affective awakening in a person's life, which constitute experiences of personal self-transcendence. These intense feelings that lift a person to new heights of awareness can be positive experiences of celebration, joy, and love, or they can be negative feelings of anger, sorrow, or pain. These inner affectional experiences present special moments of self-transcendence; they are privileged interior vehicles for experiences of transcendent integration of the self. Such moments of intense emotion and awareness, Maslow's "peak experiences," can occur in relationships with persons, ideas, memories, events, or natural scenes. Things are seen as wholes and appreciated for their own value rather than for selfish interest. Times of awe are receptive rather than active; they tend to resolve antinomies and replace inhibitions and anxieties with a sense of freedom and peace.

These experiences of wonder are eminently religious, because, in and through the concrete happening, a person is raised beyond himself to participate in a fuller enhancement of value or being. Furthermore, these human symbols of wonder dispose the person toward a deeper immersion into the unfathomable mystery of all existence. We can do no more here than uncover a few examples of such experiences in the life of Che. One such event occurred in his early travels when he lived with the lepers along the banks of the Amazon. He felt a poignant solidarity with these desperate and lonely people whom he tried to serve. After three months' work there, the patients built a raft so that Che and his companion could continue down the river. The emotion-laden scene of departure was recorded by Che: "When . . . it was my turn to speak, I was very moved. . . . It seemed dreamlike; everything was embellished by the affection and sense of brotherhood that joined all of us at that moment."[12]

His sudden decision to forgo a secure position in Venezuela and join the revolutionary movement in Guatemala was a moment of intense decision and feeling. Another incident became an experience of relief and fraternal joy when sleeping soldiers turned out to be fellow guerrillas. Che was visibly moved at the Punta del Este conference when a fisherman grabbed Guevara's arms and told him that the poor people were with him and that he must not let them down. His letter to Fidel on the occasion of leaving Cuba to open new guerrilla fronts communicates vivid brotherly emotions: "There are many things I would like to say to you and to our people . . . words cannot express . . . I embrace you with all my revolutionary fervor."[18] And finally his letter of "last embrace" to his family manifests emotions of love and concern; although his relatives may not understand him, he asks them to believe the deep feelings he holds for them.

To the subjective symbols of Che's self-transcendence, namely those of intellectual coherence and affectional wonder, must be added a third category, the images of moral decision making. How did he judge good and evil, and how did he act on these judgments? It is important to perceive Che's morality not as that of a scholar, but rather as the ethic of an activist. The morality of a "revolutionary activist" is less a matter of theory than of lived solidarity with the concrete causes of justice in an unjust situation. The general theme of Che's morality is best summed up in the striking phrase of the Cuban hero José Martí: "A real man should feel on his own cheek the blow given to another man's cheek." Guevara explicitly associated his sentiments with those of Martí, who stated: "With the poor of the earth I will cast my lot."

The pattern of Che's judgments about good and evil and his consequent actions revolve around the above-mentioned basic paradigm. Whatever contributes to personal and communal alienation is immoral and to be resisted; whatever fosters the new socialist consciousness and society, participates in truth and goodness. In this light, all forms of capitalist-imperialist exploitation and control define the domain of highest evil. Within these perimeters fall the variety of persons, events, and things that Che continually excoriated. These could be American capitalists or rapacious native bourgeoisies who used the revolution for personal gain, or the CIA's involvements in Bolivia. They could be the toadying of Latin American leaders to Uncle Sam (at Punta del Este), the profits extracted by Americans and Europeans from South American natural resources, or the Swiss bank accounts of affluent Latin elites.

The just and the good were defined by the contrary elements of the new socialist consciousness: classless solidarity, a co-operative rather than a competitive economy, participation of the people in decision making, the subordination of material incentives to social and humane motivations. These factors of Che's social morality were sharpened by the intensity of this idealist's love and hatred. The guerrilla leader was not afraid to speak of love: "Let me say, with the risk of appearing ridiculous, that the true revolutionary is guided by strong feelings of love."[14] The strength of his moral motivation can be seen by the following contrast: "Hatred [is] an element of the struggle . . . a people without hatred cannot vanquish a brutal enemy."[15] He tended to be a revolutionary purist for whom principles of ethics were to be implemented regardless of timing. This moral impulsiveness was somewhat held in check by Castro, but it also contributed to Che's blunders in the Bolivian campaign.

Yet it appears that the intense negative feelings of hatred were reserved mainly for the larger forces of oppression that impeded the revolutionary liberation of the people. Although he could also be severe with individuals, as in the execution of army spies, he frequently revealed benevolent concern for peasants and soldiers. Whenever possible, he tried to pay peasants for food. At times captured soldiers were set free, and even peasants suspected of being army informers were not harmed. In contrast to Batista's forces, Che's troops did not execute captured government soldiers. He refused to fire on positions for fear of hitting women and children. These examples are only indications that in the vigorous moral dialectic between love and hatred in Che, respect for the dignity of concrete persons was a significant quality of his life.

A crucial aspect of Che's experience of self-transcendence

through his moral decision making was his willingness to accept sacrifice and suffering to live out his convictions. It was vital for the authentic revolutionary to share the fate of victims of oppression and not just cheer them on from a safe distance. He must accompany the victim to victory or to death. He must be willing to struggle to relieve the people's suffering while taking hardship on himself. Because of his asthmatic infirmity, Che's physical sufferings were all the greater in the arduous mountain campaigns. From his Cuban "baptism of fire" at Alegría del Pío, in 1956, to his execution in the small Bolivan town of Higueras, in 1967, physical suffering was a constant part of his personal experience. He was able to integrate and elevate these infirmities into higher forms of courage and dedication.

But his spirit of sacrifice went beyond the body to embrace the psychic realm. He was willing to give up the material security, prestige, and power of his high post in the Cuban government to assume the risks of spreading his revolutionary vision to the hinterlands of the Congo and the Andes. Some have characterized this move as stemming from an irrepressible yen for adventure or from fears that he was failing in his Cuban programs and was about to lose his power. Whatever truth such evaluations may hold, they do not seem convincing as explanations of such an important move in Che's life. As Gerassi points out, ". . . he is the only example in the history of social revolutions of a man having reached the top and then voluntarily started from the bottom again."[16] An insight into the nature of sacrifice as an ascetic means of self-transformation and transcendence can be had from Che's own understanding of the term. When a man is completely dedicated to the revolutionary cause, he maintained, sacrifice is not something that depresses and diminishes him. Rather, hardship becomes a means for deepening and transforming the revolutionary's personality.

The violence of guerrilla warfare raises unavoidable problems in a treatment of Che's moral sense. Since violence implies destruction, how can it be perceived as a factor in the self-transcendence of the warrior or of his followers? In his earlier

years, Guevara studied with considerable interest the writings of
Gandhi on nonviolence as a method and as a life style. Che was
impressed by Gandhi's courage and unflinching pursuit of truth
and justice. But it was in Guatemala, in the midst of the overthrow of a left-leaning government by conservative forces, that
Che definitely resolved against the nonviolent approach. He believed that the world was full of intellectuals and conciliatory
men; for a successful revolution, however, it was necessary to
find those who would resolutely take up the gun. Speaking in
Peking, he asserted that revolution could be successfully attained
only through the armed struggle of the people. He felt that it
would be unforgivable to look only to elections to achieve power.
In this context, he was fond of citing Martí, who, in his
memorable manner, had stated: "He who furthers an avoidable
war in a country, and he who fails to further an unavoidable one,
is a criminal." Che was acutely aware that covert and overt
violence was a chief tool of oppressors; the exploited, he insisted,
could and ought to use violence at the right time.

But it is essential to recognize in assessing Che's moral attitude
on violence that it was not a good, an end in itself, but only a
method. Seeing violence as a means does not immediately justify
it. Moreover, it is cogently argued by nonviolent revolutionaries
that violence as a method is dehumanizing and counterproduc-
tive for both the victim and the victimizer. Yet the moral environment of violence is altered when it is seen as a method within a
larger context of possible results. Guevara judged that in Latin
America a freer and humane society could not be realized except
by guerrilla warfare. His main emphasis was not on destruction,
but on the creation of the new man and a new communal
consciousness. "There can be no defense of the country," he
asserted, "by the exercise of arms alone. We must defend our
country, rather, by constructing. . . ."[17] The placing of violence
into the context of resistance against tyrannical oppression does
not automatically justify it, but it does provide justifiable possibilities for its exercise.

There are moments when violent resistance constitutes the

dark side of love and a cry for human dignity. An outstanding example of taking up arms as a statement about the value of human life was the final resistance of the Jews in the Warsaw Ghetto under Nazi attack. Human beings were too precious to be summarily carted off to the ovens. Guevara's guerrilla warfare was not of the same genre as the Warsaw Ghetto's struggle. But the guerrilla was not a soldier of fortune, a hireling who disregarded human life. Che saw the guerrilla as much more than an adventurer; he was "a social reformer . . . [who] takes up weapons as the wrathful protest of the people against their oppressors; the guerrilla fights to change the social system that subjects unarmed brothers to opprobrium and poverty."[18]

The fervent Guevara was wont to extol the heroic *guerrillero* to epic proportions. But when legendary exaggerations are pruned, we are still confronted with the possibilities of genuine self-transcendence in the armed service of a just cause. For Che the authentic guerrilla had to be more than an efficient military man. He believed that the hardships of actual combat demanded that the guerrilla become a political man. His social conscience was to develop together with his military skill. The demands of guerrilla combat required a process of transcendence to a more dedicated and altruistic social consciousness. In this sense, a guerrilla could be said to participate in a religious experience as he immersed himself in conduct that led to an enhancement of personal and communal freedom.

Although I can admit the validity of Guevara's argument for violence in theory, I seriously question whether armed combat, even with the best of intentions, can of itself contribute to religious self-transcendence. The potential for dehumanization through warfare is so great, for both oppressor and oppressed, that personal and communal enhancement would at best be delayed rather than fostered. The resort to violent resistance against extreme exploitation is understandable and to some extent justifiable. It may also be the first step toward creating an environment for humanization. But individual and social experiences of authentic self-transcendence become genuinely possible only when the guns have been stilled.

I have been dealing with those aspects of Che's morality that concern active decision making about realizable goals, results attainable through human effort. Another important area of personal decision making with a special significance for self-transcendence pertains to coping with the existential challenge of death. This is the domain of the impossible, in as much as human strivings cannot eliminate the ultimate dissolution of death. Yet one's attitude in life toward finitude and morality can further or curtail healthy self-transcendence toward freedom in community. To fear death excessively or to ignore its reality are both modes of missing the possibilities for human growth that confrontation with this inevitable phenomenon can foster. Guevara had to constantly face the possibility of meeting his death in the Cuban and Bolivian campaigns. Che placed death within the perspective of his revolutionary goals. He was consciously willing to risk physical death in the struggle for a freer life for the people.

"Death rather than life as slaves. . . . Death to Yankee Imperialism. . . ."[19] is a terminating line of his revolutionary manifesto from the Bolivian mountains. These words are more than a mere rhetorical flourish; for they summarize his understanding of death. He believed that the new man was formed in the battle against the powers of oppression, which he chiefly classified as American imperial interests. He was dedicated to the destruction of this form of enslavement even if it meant his own death in the process. For the spiritual death to one's manhood under exploitive powers was a far worse condition than the termination of his physical life.

Che's attitude toward death reveals two moments of self-transcendence. In terms of the present, the revolutionary matrix of his thought makes it possible for him to transcend the paralyzing fear of death and to commit himself with unflagging vigor to the tasks at hand. Moreover, the communal sense of seeing himself as only one soldier in the great army of the proletariat provided a source of futurist transcendence through death. For his feeling of immersion in a revolutionary people gave him confidence that his work would go on after his death. "Wherever death may surprise us, let it be welcome, provided that this, our battle cry, may have reached some receptive ear and another hand may be extended to wield our weapons. . . ."[20] Present faith in the worth of the revolutionary struggle augments his courage to overcome fear and to risk death; futurist hope in the revolutionary people gives him an assurance that his own death will not be in vain. His death is elevated to a higher meaning in as much as it contributes to the betterment of humanity. Thus Che's stance toward death becomes a vehicle for transcending both fear and insignificance.

Guevara's religious experiences of self-transcendence move in the direction of the enhancement of freedom in community. Freedom and community are inseparable and correlative terms for him. His understanding of freedom is not limited to absence of destructive physical or mental constraint, although this negative aspect of freedom is contained in the whole revolutionary thrust for liberation from oppression. Freedom, as already intimated, is not synonymous with a better standard of living, although such material considerations constitute indispensable prerequisites for the realization of freedom. For Che, freedom is closely linked to a life of options for an individual to develop a new consciousness in community as well as a conduct and life style in keeping with socialist consciousness. This "fraternal attitude toward humanity" becomes the occasion for the development of human potentialities on mental, emotional, and volitional levels. Guevara's notion of freedom can perhaps best be described as the progressive humanization of individuals in community, the unfolding of a man's full promise to become whole.

In an exhortation to young Communists in Cuba, Che portrays the virtues of creativity, excellence in work, self-esteem, responsibility, independence of spirit, good example, and willingness to sacrifice for the welfare of the community. But all these qualities are seen as dimensions of becoming more human:

> This means that every Young Communist must be essentially human, so human that he responds to the best in human beings, brings out the best a man has to offer by means of work, study, and the exercise of continued solidarity with his people and with all the peoples of the world.[21]

This statement manages to catch Che's outlook concerning the humanizing direction and meaning of freedom. His understanding of the humanization of man through the revolution and life in socialist society becomes a religious experience of transcendence toward freedom. It is religious as a new attachment of man to potentials that surpass his present self and community realizations. Religion is here taken in its primal sense of refastening or tying a person to transcendent dimensions. The question of whether this movement of transcendence is a totally self-achieved phenomenon, whether it is a freedom totally contained in history or in some senses beyond history, whether it is a result in part of gratuitous giving (grace), will be taken up below in reference to Che's objective symbols of transcendence. What matters at this point is to grasp the transcendent facets of Che's freedom or humanization experience, which entails more than freedom from the negativities of oppression but also consists in a growing freedom for the positive attainments of psychic and societal transcendence.

This religious experience, the freeing of human possibilities, must be viewed in the context of community. Che's great hatred of capitalism was to a significant degree based on his interpretation of capitalism as anti-communitarian. He was convinced that this economic and cultural system engendered and fed human greed. In classic Marxist fashion, he believed that the principal cause of the alienation of man from his fellow man was the hoarding of the means of production and the subsequent classification of men in relationship to the individualistic system of concentrated ownership. By contrast, Che extolled the benefits of a socialist society, in which a collective and co-operative spirit would foster mutual sharing of goods and services. The new consciousness would be eminently communal; the common welfare would be the true criterion of achievement for any individual. The fullest expression of an individual was to be found in his dedication to the collective.[22]

It would be interesting to compare Guevara's optimism about the possibilities for human nature in community with similar assessments in the core literature of the Judeo-Christian tradition. Che was basically optimistic about socialist man, although he realized that the latter would need a social context of law and discipline. The major Hebrew documents, though they recognize the sinfulness of man, portray a positive view of human nature. The Christian gospel dialectic of sin and grace tended to emphasize the brokenness of man in need of God's redemption. Yet, early-Christian literature, in contrast to later, patristic developments, also stressed human potential for responding to the summons of the life of the beatitudes. But it is especially on the question of communitarian sharing that Guevara's polemic against the selfish individualism of capitalism echoes major orientations in Hebrew and Christian scriptures. The prophets repeatedly inveighed against the rich for hoarding resources and power at the expense of poor people. And the Christian ethic of communal, egalitarian sharing of goods and services is a dominant theme in much gospel literature. Guevara's socialist consciousness is surely closer to these traditionally religious ideals than the individualistic thrust of contemporary capitalism.

Yet Guevara's stress on the collective must be kept in a dialectical relationship with his vision of the individual's value within the community. The most important risks in his own life, the Cuban and Bolivian wars, manifest his conviction that inspired and dedicated individuals could alter the pattern of history. Although the revolutionary spirit was radically inimical to individualism, the revolution was also opposed to bringing about a dull standardization of citizens. In the socialist community, man's individual talents would ideally be liberated for their maximum flowering. In his address on revolutionary medicine, Guevara made it clear to doctors, whose profession has traditionally been a highly individualistic one, that the revolution did not intend to suppress individual talent, but to reorient it. The new task was to channel the creative abilities of all medical professionals toward the tasks of social medicine. Che advocated: ". . . the free unfolding of each man and the achievement of his most adequate utilization for the benefit of the collectivity."[23] In the light of his religious perspective, Che saw the transcendence of narrow individualism as a vital factor in the humanization of man. His freedom from alienation depended upon the overcoming of an individualism that kept man from realizing his potential in community.

The dimension of community in the personal experience of self-transcendence toward greater freedom implies of necessity the problem of balancing freedom among freedoms. A central issue of social ethics consists in protecting an individual's claims to his own rights while at the same time acknowledging the rights of others in community. The latter aspect calls for a certain limitation of the individual's rights, but the common welfare, which limits, also establishes the environment for the development of an individual's rights. Thus the rights of others in community play both a negative and a positive role in reference to the freedom claims of an individual. Guevara offers no clear solution to the problem of freedom among freedoms. On the whole, his answers to this question favor the limitation of individual rights for the sake of the collective. This emphasis on the community's rights can be observed in Che's personal efforts to protect workers in Cuba from undergoing ideological investigations in their factories. In this intervention he stressed the dignity and rights of the individual, but Guevara's official document immediately adds that each man must be utilized for the benefit of the collectivity. It is to an extent understandable that a nation such as Cuba undergoing a fundamental social revolution would experience the need to marshal the collective effort of all toward common tasks. But this direction runs the concomitant risk of abusing the individual's rights in the name of community needs. The further danger exists that the unchallenged ruling party will read its own interests as those of the people. In both eventualities the possibilities for self-transcendence are curtailed. Either the individual's creativity, honesty, and self-direction are suppressed or the people's true needs and potentials are masked and diverted. Thus an adequate resolution of the issue of freedom among freedoms is crucial for creating a milieu favorable to the transcendent religious experience.

A final element in Che's experience of community was his growing awareness of the world-wide dimensions of the liberation struggle. The success of the Cuban revolution convinced him that the time was ripe to extend rebellions to all countries in which oppression reaches unbearable levels. He adopted the colorful language of Castro in envisioning the mountain range of the Andes as "the Sierra Maestra of [Latin] America." Beyond the western hemisphere, he looked hopefully to the start of "two, three or many Vietnams . . . throughout the world."[24] The universalizing of the conflict against what he saw as oppressive powers constitutes an important part of Che's religious experience.

In great world religions there is a gradual embracing of all mankind within the salvational mission of what was originally a more exclusively chosen group. This historical pattern indicates a progression within the lived experience of a particular group of religionists, a universalizing movement revealing significant transcendence of narrow and provincial impulses. This self-transcendence is an enhancement of freedom in as much as it embraces and co-operates with a larger fellowship of humanity. Within this wider community, the possibilities for human growth are increased. Whatever conclusions may be drawn about the means that Che Guevara espoused to spread his dream, the scope of that dream was dramatic and all-embracing. It could be satisfied with nothing less than a new brotherhood of man that transcended the racial, class, and ethnic barriers that presently divide mankind.

It is important to conclude this chapter with a consideration of the religious worth of the symbols that acted as objective stimuli for Che, and finally, with the symbolic quality of his own personality. Che internalized various Marxist and revolutionary symbols that became for him inspirational lures for his intellectual, affectional and moral activity. If we examine these master images in themselves, however, a special problem arises. They seem to lack the dimension of grace; that is, of a freely bestowed gift. The symbols appear to be products of human invention only, and, as such, they could be interpreted as excluding the transcendent dimension that has traditionally been ascribed to religion. Moreover, Guevara's symbols seem to be confined to history and in no way go beyond the historically realizable. For the sake of simplifying this discussion, I will group Che Guevara's objective symbols of self-transcendence under the simple term the New People (NP). This concept includes the ideas of new socialist man and a society of changed consciousness in which the common good would be the ruling criterion. Many other facets of NP, treated throughout this chapter, need not be repeated. The important question concerns the authentic religiousness of NP.

Although the terminology of traditional religions is not employed by Che when he refers to the NP, this symbol contains many of the genuine elements of classic objective religious symbols. The NP is not the creation of any one revolutionary. It acts as a ground and gift for all their strivings. It is not an idolatrous category, because NP remains an unfinished, openended image. For Che transcendent power does not reside mainly in the revolutionary but rather in the NP. Each man's work is enhanced by participating in the life and suffering of the NP, but the latter transcends all those involved in the revolutionary struggle at any one time. In this sense the NP is an eschatological concept, a reality of the future that is not yet realized, but which influences life in the present.

This transcendent symbol of the future acts as a source of judgment on the designs of even the greatest leaders of the revolutionary cause. None of these heroes can predict the exact shape and style of the NP. The NP acts for Che Guevara as a portal through which he can glimpse and experience the further, undefinable reaches of human existence. In this sense, the NP acts as "immanent ultimacy."[25] Finally, we can say of the NP that as an eschatological symbol it is not totally confined to the historically attainable. Although revolutionaries such as Che are given to swollen rhetoric about the achievements of the Cuban rebellion, it would be an inconceivable *hybris* for such revolutionaries to announce that a particular nation had at any given stage arrived at a point of unsurpassable perfection as a socialist society. Therefore the NP becomes by definition a symbol that transcends any particular historical manifestation. For all functional purposes it is as fully eschatological as the term "Kingdom of God."

Che Guevara's objective symbol of self-transcendence, the NP, did not contain any explicit God belief. Régis Debray, commenting on the complex Che as one who could be authoritarian, introverted, and visionary, stated: "He [Che] was a mystic without a transcendent belief; a saint without a God."[26] In the following chapters on revolutionaries with explicit God beliefs we can profitably speculate on the possible pros and cons of such adherence. It could be argued, for example, that with Che the NP supplied some of the benevolent and personalizing elements that God belief provides for others. By his faith and hope in the NP, Che could experience a pledge of friendliness in the midst of an unjust and hostile universe. The corrective elements of the NP could also restrain Che's revolutionary fanaticism from going over the brink into insanity.

But the point to be made here is that Debray's assessment would be wrong if it were interpreted to mean that Guevara's lack of God belief meant a lack of religious experience. For, aside from the question of the relative merits of objective religious symbols such as God belief or NP, Che abundantly manifested an inner dynamic of self-transcendence that constitutes a religious experience at a level deeper than that of objective symbols. Yet even the status of Guevara's worldly, objective symbols, as gathered in the New People, deserve to be treated as authentically religious. In a real sense, NP may be a more valid eschatological term than the Kingdom of God. For the latter carries with it overtones of supernaturalism, of a realm completely other than the historical world. I wish to show in subsequent chapters that such traditional religious language, when used by religionists such as Berrigan and King, has acquired a new intentionality both as to content and function. It is precisely when the Kingdom of God is understood as the New People that it acts as a lure for man's deepest religious élan.

Che remained to the end of his life a servant of the NP, but in an important manner he became a mediational symbol of transcendence for others. Even in life he became a legendary figure who led the way against forces of oppression. But after his death he was transmuted into an epic hero. Fidel Castro epitomized this symbolic mythmaking in his eulogy for Che: ". . . but rarely can one say of a man . . . what we say of Che: that he was a pure example of revolutionary virtues! He constituted, through his virtues, what can be called a truly model revolutionary."[27] I am not interested in justifying these accolades but rather in the process by which a man becomes a messianic mediator for aiding the self-transcendence of others toward freedom in community.

In Guevara we can trace a movement from the personal and individualized self-experience in the early periods of his life to a less personalized and more collective self-understanding in his later years. The younger Che tended to relate his travels, encounters, and insights to himself as a unique, experiencing individual. But in his major addresses as an accomplished revolutionary, the focus changes to seeing himself as an instrument for the realization of the NP, a living symbol of a new life style and consciousness. In a sense, there is a dynamic movement in his life from the personal to the impersonal, from the inwardly oriented youth of exploits and sensitivities to the outwardly directed symbol of attractive and surpassing revolutionary virtues.

The creation of Che the symbol had already begun in his own life. It resulted from an objectification of his subjective experiences; by "depersonalizing" himself, Che could become a transcendent symbol for others. Surely the guerrillas who lived with him in the Cuban and Bolivian actions still observed many of the personalized strengths and weaknesses of a concrete man. It can even be argued that Che's self-objectification as revolutionary hero during his lifetime contributed to a dangerous arrogance toward concrete individuals and groups. For the objectified hero is less easily dissuaded in his views, nor does he investigate carefully the needs and aspirations of those he wants to enlist in the revolutionary cause. But despite these drawbacks Che had become for countless persons a transcendent revolutionary symbol. He became more than a unique person of great revolutionary stature. His martyrdomlike death at the height of revolutionary exploits projected him into a savior figure who could empower others to seek new experiences of self-transcendence toward freedom in community by the route of revolutionary strivings.

Footnotes

1. Rolando E. Bonachea and Nelson P. Valdes, eds., *Che: Selected Works of Ernesto Che Guevara* (Cambridge: MIT Press, 1969), p. 93.

2. John Gerassi, ed., *Venceremos: the Speeches and Writings of Che Guevara* (New York: Simon & Schuster, 1969), p. 393.

3. *Venceremos*, p. 91.

4. Bonachea-Valdes, p. 153.

5. *Venceremos*, p. 218.

6. *Venceremos*, p. 116.

7. Ernesto Che Guevara, *Socialism and Man* (New York: Young Socialist Alliance, 1968), p. 20.

8. Marvin D. Resnick, *The Black Beret: the Life and Meaning of Che Guevara* (New York: Ballantine Books, 1969), p. 110.

9. *Venceremos*, p. 243.

10. *Venceremos*, p. 20.

11. *Venceremos*, p. 116.

12. Martin Ebon, *Che: the Making of a Legend* (New York: New American Library, 1969), p. 20.

13. *Venceremos*, p. 411.

14. *Venceremos*, p. 398.

15. *Venceremos*, p. 422.

16. *Venceremos*, p. 21.

17. *Venceremos*, p. 211.

18. *Black Beret*, p. 237.

19. Bonachea-Valdes, p. 184.

20. *Venceremos*, p. 424.

21. *Venceremos*, p. 217.

22. Other examples of Che's anti-individualistic orientation are: ". . . you have got to be ready to sacrifice any individual benefit for the common good" (*Venceremos*, p. 105); "Isolated individual endeavor, for all its purity of ideas, is of no use, no purpose if one works alone" (*Venceremos*, p. 113).

23. Bonachea-Valdes, p. 71.

24. *Venceremos*, p. 423.

25. Cf. p. 20.

26. *Che: the Making of a Legend*, p. 173.

27. *Venceremos*, p. 438.

Bibliography

Bonachea, Rolando E. and Valdes, Nelson P. (eds.). *Che: Selected Works of Ernesto Che Guevara.* Cambridge: MIT Press, 1969.

Gerassi, John (ed.). *Venceremos: the Speeches and Writings of Che Guevara.* New York: Simon & Schuster, 1969.

Lavan, George (ed.). *Che Guevara Speaks: Selected Speeches and Writings.* New York: Merit Publishers, 1967.

Guevara, Ernesto Che. *Socialism and Man.* New York: Young Socialist Alliance, 1968.

————.*Reminiscences of the Cuban Revolutionary War.* New York: Monthly Review Press, 1968.

Scheer, Robert (ed.). *The Diary of Che Guevara.* New York: Bantam Books, 1968.

James, Daniel (ed.). *The Complete Bolivian Diaries of Che Guevara and Other Documents.* New York: Stein & Day, 1968.

Beckovic, Matija and Radovic, Dusan. *Che: A Permanent Tragedy and Random Targets.* New York: Harcourt-Brace, 1970.

Ebon, Martin. *Che: the Making of a Legend.* New York: New American Library, 1969.

González, Luís J. and Sánchez Salazar, Gustavo A. *The Great Rebel: Che Guevara in Bolivia.* New York: Grove Press, 1969.

James, Daniel. *Che Guevara.* New York: Stein & Day, 1969.

Resnick, Marvin D. *The Black Beret: the Life and Meaning of Che Guevara.* New York: Ballantine Books, 1969.

Rojo, Ricardo. *My Friend Che.* New York: Grove Press, 1968.

Sinclair, Andrew. *Che Guevara.* London: Fontana, 1970.

III - Daniel Berrigan

As the police approached to arrest Daniel Berrigan at the site of the draft-file burning in Catonsville, Maryland, on May 17, 1968, he announced: "I wanted to say 'yes' to the possibility of a human future."[1] At first glance, Berrigan, the Jesuit poet-priest, and Guevara, the guerrilla hero, would seem to have little in common. Yet their mutual passion about the possibility of a better human future marks the experience of these rebellious men. In the religious experience of Dan Berrigan many points of similarity with the experiences of Che Guevara will appear. By personality, temperament, and cultural conditioning, the two were very different. But their experiences of self-transcendence toward freedom in community bear similar nuances of dissenting religiousness. With Guevara the task was to discover in what way the worldly major was a deeply religious man; with Berrigan, the purpose will be reversed—to uncover the fundamentally worldly core of a professionally religious figure. Through Berrigan's writings and actions, I want to point out a development in him from otherworldly and ecclesiastical emphases to a religiousness that stressed possibilities for a human future.

The history and traits of Dan Berrigan need not be rehearsed at length, since he and his brother Philip have been frequently written about in relation to the celebrated trials at Catonsville, Maryland and Harrisburg, Pennsylvania. He absorbed a respect for letters and a sense of rebelliousness from his father, Thomas Berrigan, a socially progressive man for his times. At the end of high school, Dan entered the Society of Jesus, where he became a poet laureate and taught in various schools of the order. His contacts with the French worker-priest movement in the early 1950s was a significant stage in his political education. His reputation as a writer and as an inspirational personality for social action among the young grew, especially during his years as a teacher at Le Moyne College, in Syracuse. It was also there that he was increasingly labeled as a radical by the majority of his more conservative Jesuit fellows for his liturgical experimentations, modernized theology, and association with liberal sociopolitical causes.

His second trip to France, followed by travels in Communist countries in 1963 and 1964, turned the earnest liberal into an outspoken radical. His writings of this period reflect the need for a thorough reform of the church; in the spirit of John XXIII, Berrigan wanted the stodgy and ingrown Catholic Church to become the servant of the world's poor. The racial experience of Selma and the escalation of the Vietnam War in 1965 were crucial events in the radicalizing of the priest-poet. Berrigan became a leader in the Clergy and Laymen Concerned About Vietnam and thus a natural scapegoat for the hawkish Cardinal Spellman, who had him exiled to South America for his anti-war activities.

This Latin American trip, together with more involvement in peace and poverty projects on his return to the United States, was bringing to birth in Berrigan a new level of radical commitment. The way of civil disobedience, of illegal but dramatic actions, stood before him. In October 1967 Philip Berrigan and others poured blood on Selective Service files. Seven months later Daniel joined the action group by setting fire to the draft records at Catonsville. His greatest national notoriety came when, convicted and sentenced, he became a fugitive for four months. Before his capture on Block Island, Rhode Island, and imprisonment at Danbury, Connecticut, Berrigan became a special source of embarrassment to the government by appearing in various media to protest the war. By attempting to escape the penalties for his acts of civil disobedience, Berrigan was consciously raising nonviolent protest to new forms of dramatic protest. He believed this unprecedented style of resistance to be a necessary technique for communicating his message against the war makers. He and his brother had chosen "to be powerless criminals in a time of criminal power—chosen to be branded as peace criminals by war criminals."[2] More recently he has been implicated by association with the charges brought against Philip and others in the Harrisburg conspiracy case for planning the destruction of heating systems in Washington and the kidnaping of presidential adviser Henry Kissinger.

In *No Bars to Manhood*, Berrigan comes close to summarizing the present orientation of his life and hopes: "We saw our action as a social method of achieving a future for man."[3] Berrigan does not see himself as a formulator of final solutions to the dilemmas of history. Rather, his self-image is that of a radical visionary who beholds the possibilities of a new man in a new society. As his vision becomes more integrated, he realizes that war, racism, and poverty are interrelated; with the creation of a new heart and consciousness in man and community there is hope. Berrigan's personal development of inner and outer motivating images toward this new human integration is the core of his religious experience.

Dan Berrigan is a personality of deep sensitivity, candor, and courage. His sensitivity is seen in his poetic gifts, as well as in his sensibilities about social evils. Part of this sensitivity is marked by a profound respect for human life that he felt was so abused by the war in Indochina. He spoke of his own graduation from liberal innocence about American destructiveness in war when he sheltered a child during a Hanoi air raid: "In my arms fathered/ in a moment's grace, the messiah/ of all my tears. I bore, reborn/ a Hiroshima child from hell."[4] This episode expresses well his acute sensitivity to the value of life and the evil of war. Another aspect of this sensitivity is his steadfast adherence to nonviolence as the most humane and fruitful style of living. Even his protest actions against government property were carefully circumscribed to avoid injury to persons.

A candid simplicity has always endeared Berrigan to his friends, who form an essential support family for his gregarious bent. His strong loyalty to the Jesuit Order reveals a response of gratitude for the nurture and stimulation he has received from close friends and associates. The relationship to his brother, Philip, has been the closest source of motivation for him, especially in making decisions to perform risky anti-war actions. This same simplicity joined to a playful, maverick strain, has also been a source of criticism from more prosaic Jesuits and others. The candid non-conformist disconcerts the traditionalist and the legalist.

His courage to take painful and risky stands has produced, especially in recent years, a twofold reaction from others. For one group, Berrigan's consistency between word and deed ". . . bring[s] us to our senses and restore[s] our moral sensibilities."[5] Others are repelled by illegal actions and "the self-righteous moralism [that] . . . simply will not tolerate the immorality of those who dare to disagree with him."[6] Such positive and negative judgments, while always attendant on the celebrated man who stands against the tide, are ultimately reactions to courageous gestures. Whether the latter be wise or good is a judgment that only history or subsequent events will clarify, but the element of personal courage evidenced in the religious experience of Dan Berrigan is undeniable.

His inner symbols of self-transcendence—coherence, wonder, and morality—can be unified by an over-all descriptive summary of Berrigan's religious experience. It is an experience of *prophetic* (words and acts) *suffering* love against the powers of *death* for the sake of *life* (freedom) in *community*. By examining each of the underlined elements, the main interior motivating images of his spiritual life can be studied in both his extensive writings and in his activities. These inner symbols taken together form a oneness of feeling and conduct in the person of Berrigan. The division of his writings and other deeds into categories is only a hermeneutical device for analysis. In some phases of Berrigan's religiousness elements of coherence will be uppermost, at other times the quality of wonder or morality will be stressed. But, most often, all these factors are intermingled with varying intensity in the unity of his life.

Dan Berrigan's personal experience of self-transcendence toward freedom in community also reveals an important movement toward more overtly worldly concerns and involvements. Most of this study will concentrate on the later Berrigan, who from the mid-1960s became a more "worldly" man. But I shall also attempt to show by contrast with earlier works the progression of his thought and action in the direction of immediate social ends within history. It will also be important to inquire into the significance of his objective symbols of self-transcendence: explicit God belief and of the use of traditional Christian symbols. Both the subjective and the objective symbols of self-transcendence in Berrigan point to an eminently this-worldly spirituality whose overarching concern is the attainment of the fullest life for persons in this world.

Berrigan's supernatural language, while pointing to realms of mystery that transcend the present situation, is frequently a code for speaking with dramatic intensity about this-worldly matters. In Berrigan, both the internal and external symbols of self-transcendence are vitally unified in his own concrete, personal involvements. Throughout his later works there appear a basic disdain for and a guilt about hypocritical separation between words and deeds. This desire to coalesce all the motivating symbols of his life into his own body-person was already in evidence in an early poetic statement: "Your paint be blood, your canvas, you."[7] From this aspiration he rarely faltered.

The *prophetic* dimension of the Judaeo-Christian tradition

forms an important category of Berrigan's poetic and prose reflection. In an earlier book of essays, he developed the traits of Hebrew prophets who had special messages for the needs of the contemporary church. His meditation on Jeremiah and Ezekiel could now be applied to himself. He saw the faults of the prophets: impatience with the weaknesses and distinctions of others, overly impulsive courage, and a tendency to oversimplify. Yet he affirms the necessity for the prophets' passion for truth, with its unconcern for amenities and temporizing. Not only did political and economic areas need the prophetic voice, but also the renewal of the church demanded it.[8] But the Berrigan of the late fifties saw the prophet as obedient to and at the service of the church. His prophetic emphasis was still mainly church-oriented, with a strong sense of acquiescence to ecclesiastical authority. Although in later years he would maintain loyalty to the church institution, Berrigan would become much more severely critical of the church for its failure to serve the needs of the world, especially in matters of peace, race, and poverty.

Ten years after *The Bow in the Clouds,* his view of prophecy has changed from seeing the New Testament prophet as a voice for the church to seeing him as a voice for the world. His later sense of prophetism also demonstrated an independence of action in secular matters that he would not have previously exercised. The Berrigan who went obediently to Latin America when ordered by his superiors in 1965 would most likely not have co-operated with church officials had they ordered him out of hiding from the FBI in 1971. During these four fugitive months he conducted a series of interviews with the psychiatrist Robert Coles. In these exchanges Berrigan describes his life venture as a prophetic one of living at the edge with jeopardy in order to prod the world to question its inhumanity.

Berrigan the prophet challenges men to break away from their unfreedoms. In our present epoch of technology at the murderous service of the cold-war mentality, he views prophecy as more needed than ever. But it has to be a prophecy immersed in the experience of the world in order to speak out of real knowledge and compassion. In a poem about the waters of baptism, Berrigan gives eloquent expression to his own desire to live a prophetic life:

> Pray; holy waters never
> reduce your untamed heart.
> . . . to drift sidewise
> in deaf waters, blind,
> safe as stone.
> Fisher, saviour, save from that.[9]

In the same collection he grieves over the dearth of prophets: "and no one walks waters."[10] A worldly-directed prophetism comes through his "Suburban Prayer." He asks for ". . . grace, oppositions, stymyings/ sand in our pet gears/ a bubble in the cozy blood"; all these images denote the prophet who would finally "Marry us off, lonely girls/ to Harlem and Asia" and have us "celebrate in the haunted house, the world."[11] Again, the world, not the church, is the place of celebration through prophetic involvement; the good and evil spirits are to be met in that haunted house.

During the past few years Berrigan's prophetic spirit has become more radical as he has taken nonviolent steps to put his body in the way of the war machine at the price of personal jeopardy. It was not enough to exhort suburbanites to an increased measure of social consciousness. Nor was it satisfactory to make occasional safe gestures of protest. "To be radical is habitually to do things which society at large despises."[12] After his visit to Hanoi to effect the release of captured U.S. pilots, he felt more deeply than before the price that prophecy would exact:

> Take up, take up
> the bloody map of the century.
> The long trek homeward begins
> into the land of unknowing.[13]

The general apathy and self-righteousness of America concerning Vietnam made it a land of unknowing, which the prophet had to awaken by doing such despised things as burning sacred federal property of draft records. This prophetic desecration would make him a felon in the eyes of conventional justice. It would land him in prison, where only the most radical fare would nourish his "prophetic guts": "our diet decreed by our own prophetic guts—the prison poems of Ho/ the sayings of Chairman Jesus."[14]

The fugitive Berrigan of 1970 was driven by his prophetic spirit to a life on the edges of church and society. In hiding he had discovered a new mode of speaking the good news in an empty landscape and of resisting "false, corrupting, coercive, imperialist policy."[15] Berrigan's prophetic experience to this point in his life had taught him that the initial outcry against an action by church or state may be a clear indication of the act's rightness. The prophetic stance, therefore, forms a key aspect of Dan Berrigan's experience of self-transcendence. Concrete prophetic engagement depicts his own self-image within the broader pattern of coherence symbols that give meaning to his life. As prophet, he is the subject of the deep emotions and affections of his poetry and actual life; his moral decisions are also dictated from a prophetic standpoint. This stance forms the personal basis of all other inner symbols of self-transcendence in the religiousness of Dan Berrigan.

Berrigan's prophetic stance is endowed with a particularly outstanding sense of *redemptive suffering*. The prophet is called upon to suffer within himself the misunderstandings and opposition of the dominant culture. Moreover, he will suffer because of his concrete solidarity with the poor and downtrodden; the prophet's life is a sham if he is not closely associated with the weak and needy. Yet these classic traits of prophetic suffering take on distinctive nuances in Berrigan's writings. In his earlier works, suffering is treated in an abstract and more narrowly religious way. As Berrigan's life becomes politically radicalized through his own protest actions, his outlook on prophetic suffer-

ing is concretely related to his own person, and the context of
the suffering widens to embrace humanity beyond the limited
perspectives of an earlier period. The general direction of this
movement from the abstract to the concrete, from a particularist
to a universalist context, reveals the fundamentally humanistic
and worldly essence of Berrigan's religiousness.

As seen in *The Bow in the Clouds,* suffering is portrayed as a
principal way by which the Christian strives to make life available. Berrigan warns against pessimism among Christians who
consciously embrace redemptive suffering; for he reminds the
reader that suffering in the battle against the forces of death is a
road to victory and new life. But his discussion of suffering in
this context tends to be abstract and church oriented. His
treatment of the subject of suffering is marked by the typical
generalities of the priest who, well versed in contemporary
biblical theology, gives spiritual exhortation to nuns. The talk
about sufferings seems distant and safe. It is enshrouded in the
familiar holy language of "church militant" and "Christian
apostolate." In a similar manner, his discussion about the sufferings of Christ as necessary for resurrectional victory is a pale
treatment of a much repeated historical theme; the traditionally
religious language of this essay is oriented toward a past event
in history. Suffering is robbed of its sense of worldly immediacy and intensity.

With the sudden blow of his summary exile to Latin America
in 1965, suffering became for Berrigan a very personal and immediate question related to his struggle to accept the rude
mandate of church officials. Berrigan's sensitivity to the sufferings of people can be found throughout his poetry, as in these
reflections on the French-Algerian war: ". . . World spins
like a headless top,/ butchers put up their shutters,/ Caesar in
dreams sucks red thumbs clean."[16] But his desire "to stand
in that picture, to kneel and drink at a god's fountainhead"[17]
only becomes a reality for him when his actions against the
American involvement in Vietnam bring the sufferings of exile
and later imprisonment into his own life.

As his aesthetic sensibilities became more attuned to the sufferings of black people in America, he became convinced that only the pain of the black experience could redeem and revive the white Lazarus bound in the cerements of his prejudice. His reflections on black suffering have the immediacy and concreteness of being prayers extracted painfully from Berrigan's own white skin. In the late 1960s, his meditation on the sufferings of war are no longer distant abstractions about the gospel experience alone. Newness of life and hope would pass into our history through contemporary sufferings; the passwords for seeding hope and flowering peace are: Hiroshima, Dresden, and Dachau.

His thoughts about the sufferings of Ho Chi Minh's exile and imprisonment as twin focuses of inward renewal become personal reflections on his own similar experiences. After the personal jeopardy into which the Catonsville incident placed him, the cross of suffering was no longer the terminology of familiar liturgies and pious sermons. It was now rooted in the worldly commitments of his own flesh: "We have chosen to say, with the gift of our liberty, if necessary of our lives, the violence stops here, the death stops here, the subversion of truth stops here, the war stops here."[18] In his dialogue with Robert Coles he talks about the personal importance for him to taste and feel the sufferings of Third World people. Such tangible sharing of the lot of the oppressed is at the core of the liberation revolution.

Berrigan's sense of prophetic suffering is not a masochistic need to inflict pain on himself for ascetic purposes. His writings, with their deep appreciation of and reveling in life, offer a corrective to such individualistic pursuits. Nor are his sufferings undertaken for the sake of church reform in the sense of organizational or liturgical renewal in ecclesiastical matters. Although he remains a churchman, his purpose as a priest is to draw the church into the wider arena of life, into those areas of costly service through which not just church reform but human reform may be realized. But he could not bring about this revolutionary goal of reform until he realized through his own sufferings what it might cost to be a Christian. A portion of this cost he could only discover as a consequence of making his prophetic gestures against the forces of death, which for him were epitomized in the murderous direction of the American war machine. Part of the cost was to be cut off from the normal privileges of community and citizenship, to have to live and perhaps die outside the walls. He would become a felon for pouring blood and fire on murderous licenses.

The danger of posturing, of self-glorification through suffering, is always a danger, especially for the celebrated person. It is impossible to know what degree of martyr complex invades even the best of men. But Berrigan's personal understanding of suffering appears to be overwhelmingly oriented toward the humanizing of life in society. Suffering is not for itself, but it becomes in the revolutionary struggle an enlightening and transforming byproduct of prophetic involvement. Berrigan's "yes" to a more humane community of life and love necessitated a purposeful acceptance of the pain and hardship as part of the prophetic stance against a mighty established order that he saw as entrenched in the ways of death. In *The Dark Night of Resistance,* a book of lyrical reflections related to St. John of the Cross, Berrigan speaks of deepening of his own spiritual life through suffering. This book, written on the run from the FBI, is an interior chronicle of the suffering resister who enters the darkness of his own night as a fugitive felon.

The inner symbols of meaning, affection, and morality for Berrigan center around his prophetic and suffering stance toward the *powers of death.* Since the middle 1960s he has clustered these death forces around the war-making direction of American life, especially in reference to the Vietnam War. He was convinced that the nation's vision of life had been shrouded by cold-war passions linked to an efficient technology. This cold-war technology expressed an ultimate contempt for man, and it led to the Neanderthal alternatives of either total destruction or a perilous arms race. Like Martin L. King, Jr., Berrigan claimed that the great issues of race and poverty were closely related to the leading problem of a war-oriented nation. It was part of the crime of war that the poor and racially disadvantaged were most abused, while the affluent became richer.

He saw America confronted with the incredible phenomenon of the white Westerner who hired blacks to kill Orientals and to be killed protecting the white man's interests. The latter's power was such that we could create a "vicarious executioner and [a] vicarious corpse."[19] An essentially military nation was condemned to be a walking zombie devoid of authentic human community. For the material and mental resources of such a country would be enslaved to the war mind, which lacked either conscientious protest or creative alternatives. Churches could seemingly be at peace with Hiroshima and racism. The Pentagon became the home of the real enemy because it directed the cadence and momentum of the American death dance. All the exorcisms of fasting, demonstration, and civil disobedience conducted by the resisters were attempts to cast out from the American zombie the spirit of death.

A special suffering for Berrigan was the realization that the institutional Church had either joined or let itself be drawn into the dance of death. Official religion took no risks with its own survival and security; it remained a silent and docile accomplice of the war makers. His deep sense of evangelical demands made it very painful for Berrigan to see institutional religion at the service of the war machine. In his reflections on the mysticism of John of the Cross, Berrigan discloses a paradox in his own spirituality. To struggle against the powers of death in society he had to die to the Great Church that supported the Great Society. His bold challenge of a war-prone state also marked a significant break in traditional American Catholic loyalty and subservience to the aims of government. He wondered whether military chaplains had compromised their responsibility to speak judgment on the military state that nourished and domesticated them. Did they have to clear the spirit of Christ with Pentagon authorities?[20] For Berrigan the great failing of the church was its sin of silence.

The death forces had significant effects on the development of human personalities. Berrigan's reflections on the American flyers released by Hanoi form piercing tableaux of deadened consciences. He describes the enormous deformative power of militarism and nationalism on the released officers. These men had been thoroughly trained to be thoughtful, respectable but conscientiously uncritical killers who would be facilely integrated into the modern state, church, and family. Of one of the pilots, Berrigan says that obedience was his obituary. And he refers to these words of a major as the most ominous of all: "I am an Army career man. Any least indication of the will of my superior is a command to me."[21]

> Every day, every day for three years
> efficient as a madman's
> three-year plan
> for renewal of the earth
> the bombers go out
> renewing the earth.[22]

Such were the men who could make death a way of life, who could fill Hanoi's museums with a history of death.

Against these personalities trained in the school of death, Berrigan was learning by increasingly concrete stages to form himself into a resister of the death forces. The high point of his testimony in the Catonsville trial is permeated with an intense consciousness of the deathly environment that surrounded him and that provoked him to fashion modes of countereducation. He explained to the court that he was trying to be concrete about death. An American high school lad's anti-war self-immolation had made Berrigan understand in a new way the power of death in the modern world. He had to speak and act against death because that boy's death was being multiplied a thousand times in the Land of Burning Children. For it was in Vietnam that he deeply experienced the tragedy of children destroyed by war. He could hear "the blackened hands beating/

the box of death for breadth."[23] Berrigan's cry before the court summarizes his poignant awareness of the forces of death: "How many indeed must die before our voices are heard? How long must the world's resources be raped in the service of legalized murder?"[24] In this time of death, Berrigan was completely dedicated to the formation of a new kind of man. These were the resisters who worked for social change and overcame death in the name of life and gentleness and community and unselfishness. Here we see the paradox of the new man according to Berrigan. Only by assimilating into his person an indomitable and courageous gentleness could the new man put down the death forces: "erase with your mouth to mouth respiration/ the mortician smile of death."[25]

The prophetic struggle against the forces of death in the dynamic of self-transcendence is for the purpose of releasing the human potential for *fuller life*. Life for Berrigan is almost synonymous with the enhancement of freedom in individuals and in community. This theme has been consistently central to Berrigan's thought over the years. It was expressed in his definition of a Christian as one who strives manfully to make life available.[26] The same motif inspires his activities in the later years of political protest: "There is one gift, life itself; . . . the cry of childbirth, the last breath of the dying. Love, love life. Die, loving life."[27] Yet, within this consistent orientation, an important shift of emphasis should be noted. In earlier works, Berrigan took pains to show that authentic life, while a worldly reality, was principally to be found in Christianity. Life in the world is judged good, but the right use of this life is a specifically Christian invitation. The unbeliever tends to be guided by less noble motives; without the churchly correctives, he is prone to an idolatry and abuse of life. Again, he maintained that apart from Christ, men often became masters of new tyrannies over life in the world.

In "Please, Please" a significantly altered and broadened perspective about life can be noted: "Death-ridden people, the cure of the world lies within the world; only life is the healer of

life."[28] It would be wrong to say that the contemporary, radicalized Berrigan has rejected the specifically Christian or churchly
inspiration for his acts to enhance life forces in the world. But
he has in a noteworthy way expanded the context of his religious
experience. He has moved from a kind of Christian provincialism
that claimed that it alone had a life-giving message for the
world. He no longer held that to have life deeply and authentically the world must follow the dictates of the church. His later
religious experience derives more immediately from life itself,
from the world as a bountiful source of healing and renewal.
From a churchly humanism of self-aggrandizing particularism,
Berrigan progressed to a religious humanism in which "only
life is the healer of life."

Berrigan's understanding of life is intimately linked to his
view of freedom. Mature religion had essentially to do with
freeing one's person to be as creative as possible in life. He saw
that Christians were especially guilty of the suppression of
freedom through various forms of overcontrol. Berrigan's awareness of the importance of freedom for life growth was intensified by a convergence of factors in the 1960s. The progressive orientation of Vatican II had accentuated the need of
personal freedom for authentic religious development in a church
that for centuries had restricted the freedom if its adherents
in the name of tradition, security, and salvation. During the
same period the tragedy of Vietnam brought home to Berrigan
the extent to which the United States slavishly committed its
human and material resources to deeds of killing. The military
posture of the nation gravely limited the freedom to create the
new man and society that Berrigan envisioned. The unfreedoms
of both church and society landed heavily on Berrigan's personal
life when superiors exiled him and the court imprisoned him
for anti-war activities.

Yet these same pressures taught him that the core of freedom
consisted in the inner ability of a man to choose creative alternatives even in the face of great opposition. A religion could
be judged worthwhile if it fostered these humanly creative al-

ternatives. In his parable "My Son John" Berrigan brings out how the concrete living of alternatives is the road to growth of freedom. When the boy in the story had experienced the life of men in the back yard and could bring the message to the front yard, he had learned how to become a man.[29] The participatory experience of others' freedoms and non-freedoms had raised new questions, stimulated new answers. The boy could never be the same again; but the freer person, while a hope, was also a threat to the status quo. He warns people to beware of a free man. The boy of the parable was also Dan Berrigan, who had to choose among alternatives toward his own freedom.

It took four years of inner struggle for him to make the major choices among alternative ways to combat the war machine. He was willing to pay the significant price that is attached to gaining the freedom to face one's times. But this freedom for Berrigan is paradoxical. It was not those who glory in belonging to the "free world" who are really free; most of these people were not even aware of their unfreedoms. Nor were they necessarily free who live outside of jails: "Who is free anyway, and who is unfree, given the world—given the Church?"[30] Thus paradox exists in Berrigan's spirituality that the freedom leading to fuller life must pass through the darkness and pain of confrontation with the death forces of unfreedom. In his own life as a peace-making resister he learned the great cost of becoming free at the moment when his civil liberties were being curtailed. It was such freedom that made it possible for him to choose another way of life than the death of brothers. Through gestures of paradoxical freedom, he encouraged other resisters to raise the ante of courageous action.

The symbols of intellectual coherence, affectional wonder, and moral decision making thus far considered would be incomplete and ethereal without an environment of *incarnate community*. Prophetic suffering against the powers of death for the sake of freer life, as a description of Berrigan's religiousness, must be set in the all-pervasive milieu of his communal consciousness. I have indicated a movement in Berrigan's spirituality away from otherworldliness toward a religiousness of this-worldly concern and involvement. Yet there is a striking consistency through all his writings of a strong sense of incarnateness in human community, which deepens and becomes all-embracing in later works. Berrigan's desire to live fully in the world community is emphatic whether he is discussing the church or an individual Christian.

When Berrigan deals with ecclesiology, he is usually engaged in developing ideas that counterbalance the dichotomous and supernaturalist piety that so deeply informs the religious life of his own Catholic community. The church was swallowed by this past and was unrelated to a humanizing present. He urges that the whole realm of the sacred be defined in terms of the incarnation of God in creation and human history.[31] He inveighs against a form of Cartesian Christology that long permeated the thinking of the church; the mystery of the world must be seen as the mystery of Christ. World issues are Christian issues. The purpose of the church is to be at the service of the poor, as was the Christ. His Christ has "flowered in man's flesh"[32]; a Christ of whom the poet says: "I see you in the world."[33]

The church's sacramental life makes sense only in terms of its value for fashioning and furthering worldly community. Baptism is seen as a consecration to the world, to social and personal change, to community. The Eucharist is a food for the building of the body of mankind, as opposed to angelic interpretations of this sacrament. He could not see himself dying to vindicate the truth of the Eucharist, he tells Robert Coles, except in a very new way. In this sense, Eucharist means that man is of value, a person not to be degraded or violated. He contrasts the kind of enervated worship of Sunday Christians with the real liturgies that coalesce when human beings open their hearts to one another ". . . in the fires of social protest, their hands warmed by a passion for human justice."[34] In his introduction to *They Call Us Dead Men*,

William Stringfellow could remark that this book was not about religion in the typical sense but about life in the world.

In the life of an individual, Berrigan perceives religiousness in that person's lived experience of becoming more human in a worldly community. He notes that two of his models for conduct, Alfred Delp and Dietrich Bonhoeffer, conceived of true religiousness as being simply men among men. This human religiousness implied living truthfully in the world; the condition of truthful life meant taking the risk of prophetic suffering. The true life of faith would foster a passion for justice, but such existence in turn would exact a cost and a purification in and through the world. To be Christian meant to Dan Berrigan to live human life at depth, to be faithful to the times. He was suspicious of celibates who spoke of love but who disdained contact with human beauty.

Berrigan's vision of community also became more concretely universal through his experiences of recent years. As an extension of Christian universalism, he had always hoped for a human community of wide brotherhood and compassion. But his specific involvements with the racially and culturally other, at home and abroad, allowed him to clothe with intense poetic feeling his previous general hopes for human fellowship. His experience in the release of the flyers from Hanoi revealed concretely to him the narrow confines by which the pilots circumscribed their sense of community. They constricted their view of human community to immediate relations or friends. By contrast, Berrigan expressed his wider vision of human community and the latter's significance for his own experience of self-transcendence in "Prayer for the Big Morning": "People my heart/ with the living . . . their sight healing/ my eyes foreclosing night."[85]

We have explored the key symbols in Berrigan's religiousness of inner coherence, wonder, and morality under rubrics that are more familiarly a part of his own language: prophet, suffering, life, and community. At every stage of this discussion, the emotions of wonder break through, especially in his poetry. Berrigan's ethical posture follows a recurring pattern among the revolutionaries under study. Like Guevara, Berrigan displays a moral outlook of critical judgment on the evils visited upon the poor and the weak by the wealthy and powerful. It is an intense social morality, nuanced by the specific concerns of a North American about the wrongs of racism and war. It is almost impossible to find in Berrigan traces of the older individualistic Catholic morality so prevalent until quite recently.

But a very important point of difference between Guevara and Berrigan relates to the question of violent and nonviolent means. Berrigan's morality remains deeply and consistently influenced by the nonviolent perspectives of Gandhi and King. Berrigan understands the nonviolent method of moral action to be superior in principle and practice. For him Gandhi's life and death represent a new method in human history over against the prevalent law of violence stemming from the race's animal past. The nonviolent way, associated with Jesus and Gandhi, incorporates a relatively new law, that of love, even for enemies. Berrigan holds that such a morality is in principle more humanizing, more conducive to establishing communities of life. He compares the death of Che with that of King in terms of popular impact. For Berrigan, Che's death had less influence on the "apolitical ignorant peoples" than that of King, because the former was the killing of an antagonist, the latter was the killing of an innocent man.[36] While this argument is not really convincing, Berrigan's morality of nonviolence retains a great inspirational power for those who protest against the deeds of a violent nation.

Although Berrigan does not assume a stance of violence, he does not condemn it in an unqualified way. He shows understanding of defensive violent resistance among oppressed people toward their oppressors. "I condemn only those who are neither for one thing or the other, who knowing what is going on, do nothing while they call upon religion, prudence and common sense."[37] He counsels the Weathermen to judge carefully of the use of violence, even against property, because: ". . . we are to strive to become such men and women as may, in a new world, be nonviolent."[38] He shows keen awareness of the covert violence of those in power. Yet, precisely in a time of violence, he urges the way of nonviolence, new ways of dealing with Eichmanns.[39] Berrigan conceives of his life as a summons to enter a profound form of nonviolent humanitarianism.

Nonviolent resistance implied for Berrigan's morality the possibility of civil disobedience. At Catonsville, he maintained that one could not indefinitely obey the law while social conditions deteriorated. Moreover, he placed his disobedience to law within the American heritage whereby good men acted outside the law when the times demanded it. Although the risk of self-deception is always present when a man appeals to a higher law, conscience, especially of one trained in nonviolent sensitivities, could not be denied. Moreover, Berrigan's conscience about the evils of the American involvement in Vietnam was upheld by a growing consensus of his fellow countrymen. Finally, his attempt to escape capture by law officials was itself seen by Berrigan as a dramatic moral statement against a government that was committing the massive crimes of war.

His nonviolent civil disobedience was part of an action-oriented morality. The Catonsville and subsequent actions seemed to release him from a long sense of guilt for being like so many liberals who "even as they declare for peace, their hands reach out . . . in the direction of their comforts. . . ."[40] He was sickened by such a wasting disease of normalcy. His action-prone ethic was geared to communicate a sense of crisis to others. But conscientious action itself was also the locus from which a genuinely concrete as opposed to abstract morality could be developed. It was through ethical action that he could experience the immanent and worldly demands of his religiousness: "I could not announce the gospel from a pedestal. I must act . . . sharing the risks and burdens and anguish."[41]

All the dimensions of Berrigan's religiousness discussed to this point depict a constant process of personal self-transcendence toward greater freedom in community. This self-transcendence is the core of his spirituality. In an implicit manner it is expressed repeatedly in the key symbols of his thought and life style. At times this movement toward fuller, richer human experiences is explicitly referred to as transcendence. The master images of his writings frequently express themes of moving from death to life, from darkness to light, from the impersonal to the interrelated, from sadness to joy, from despair to hope, from pain to healing, from sin to forgiveness. This process of transcendence is not naively optimistic, as if it were moving in a linear direction in which everything was getting better and better. It is rather a dialectical process of living that manifests high and low points, moments of advance and of regression, of personal becoming and decline.

The crucial point in all this is that Berrigan's religious experience, like that of Che Guevara, is fundamentally a human experience of this-worldly transcendence. For Berrigan it is finally a question of "being in the world transcendently."[42] Each high point in the geography of his spiritual journey depicts a special moment in a continuing process of inner *metanoia,* of openness to and experience of the mystery of living in the world transcendently. The later periods of this personal growth are marked by the need to express the transcendent mystery of existence through ethical gestures of justice and love. The Catonsville actions and the fugitive period are concrete symbolic instances of Berrigan's imperative to experience mystery in worldly acts. As his spiritual life became increasingly political, however, he recognized the need to be challenged and for a willingness to change, lest his prophecy turn into dogmatic fanaticism.

Berrigan's objective symbols of transcendence, which appear to be traditionally religious and otherworldly, present a special problem. Although the inner dynamic of his spirituality moved in an increasingly worldly direction, the fact remains that Berrigan explicitly embraces the language of God belief, and, as a Jesuit priest, his life is surrounded by churchly images. Thus God and church can stand for collective objective symbols that include the rest of his expressly religious idioms. It would amount to a distortion of Berrigan's religiousness to deny that explicit religious symbols acted as objective formative and motivational images in his life. What I want to ask, however, is a question about the intentionality or purpose of his objective religious symbols.

The intentionality of Berrigan's God and Christ language is eminently this-worldly. This language is more individually personalized than Guevara's "the New People," but the direction of meaning of Berrigan's symbols is not very different. For him "God" and "Christ," however these may be nuanced in a particular Christian tradition, are essentially words that point to the creative sources of life for men in community. These traditional religious terms are code words for Berrigan's central this-worldly concern, that is, the enhancement of human life in community, so clearly defined in the foregoing discussion of his inner symbols of transcendence. The personalized God language should not distract from the intentionality of these terms: "O be YOURSELF supersensible/ available/ overflow/ LIFE!"[43] In this especially visionary poem, Berrigan's overriding concern is not about God or Christ in a supernaturalist sense, but rather about life as it is affected by the issues of race, war, and poverty.

Again, let me attempt to be clear. Berrigan believes in God and in Christ as a special mediator of transcendent reality. But the more important question concerns the meaning of this language in terms of the whole context of Berrigan's life activities and commitments. What is he really interested in, or what does he want to happen, when he uses explicitly religious terminology? When he calls upon Christ, the intentionality of the prayer manifests hope for a peaceful human future: "Into our history, pass! Seed Hope. Flower Peace."[44] Before the court at Catonsville, Berrigan clearly expressed the relationship between his religious beliefs and his controversial actions. But it would be a mistake to interpret this linking of political action and religious tenets in an ahistorical way, as though Berrigan's main interest lay with God or Christ in some realm beyond history. His God and Christ language attests to his faith in a benevolent presence and power for good in the world. Moreover, this mysterious power is even personified in the traditional mode. But what Berrigan, like Guevara, intends by faith in a mysterious power beyond the self is the creation of the new man in a community of life.

Just as Berrigan's God language is a way of talking about human life in a context less stunted by the death forces, so his church language should be seen as an objective symbol system referring to the building of broader and deeper human community. This understanding of church in the broadest sense is the result of a growth in Dan Berrigan. We can gain a clearer picture of this progression in his symbol system by examining two books, written a decade apart. In *The Bow in the Clouds* (1961) and in other, earlier works, he sees a man's rebirth into the church through baptism as a culminating point of new responsibility in community. Although he is ever conscious of the church's role to serve the world, the ecclesiastical body remains the community toward which men are called. In *No Bars to Manhood* (1970), Berrigan's view of church connotes a far more universal sense of community. Over the nine-year span his emphasis moves from God's covenant with man, to man's brotherhood with man. He does not reject the first covenant, nor does he deny his own need to be in communion with a specific church tradition for the sake of past and future orientation.

But increasingly man's knowledge and fulfillment of himself as a *man* is Berrigan's chief concern; rather than employ the churchy language of ecclesiology, he talks about man realizing his manhood. He is reflecting his own experience of rebirth into a still broader church community, a new order and a new church beyond the confines of the traditional Christian community. To realize this universal fellowship, men are called upon ". . . to free the ghetto, to disobey the law, to disavow the race, to surpass the religion."[45] He now states flatly that he has no interest in internal Catholic questions unless these issues bear on the church's stand concerning freedom and justice in the world.

In his earlier writings, Berrigan portrayed the Christian church as the soul of the world. Recently he has come to see all men from whatever tradition who pursue truth, justice, and peace with conviction as the soul of the world. For Berrigan the symbol of the church has transcended the bounds of Catholicism and of Christianity to embrace a world community. As with Guevara, Berrigan's view of the new society or the new church constitutes a symbol with positive and negative dimensions. As a future possibility, it sustains his hope and prophetic action. Yet this symbol indicates a longed-for reality that he cannot fully encompass or manipulate. In this sense it acts as a critical symbol against the temptation of the prophet to define the future community and to fanatically compel men into his own version of it. Every vision, he asserts, ought to have doubt cast on it. For, as a future possibility, it always remains an open-ended symbol.

The subjective and objective symbols of Berrigan's religiousness reveal a person of sensitivity and courage who is moving from traditional understandings of religion to one that is at once more universal and humanistic. His personal experience of self-transcendence toward freedom in community is seen in his prophetic words and suffering deeds against the death powers for the sake of life in community. The objective symbols of God and church also manifest the worldly direction of his religious experience. The pilgrimage of his life from progressive church reformer to radical world prophet embodies the insight of Dietrich Bonhoeffer that religious men are becoming something more than religious; they are becoming men.

Footnotes

1. Francine du Plessix Gray, *Divine Disobedience* (New York: Alfred A. Knopf, 1970), p. 47.

2. New York *Times*, August 12, 1970, p. 1.

3. Daniel Berrigan, *No Bars to Manhood* (New York: Doubleday & Co., 1970), p. 35.

4. Daniel Berrigan, *Night Flight to Hanoi* (New York: The Macmillan Co., 1968), p. 57.

5. Robert McAfee Brown, "The Berrigans, Signs or Models?" *Holy Cross Quarterly*, 4:1 (January 1971), p. 42.

6. Andrew M. Greeley, "Phrenetic?" *Holy Cross Quarterly*, 4:1 (January 1971), p. 17.

7. Daniel Berrigan, *Time Without Number* (New York: The Macmillan Co., 1957), p. 4.

8. Daniel Berrigan, *The Bow in the Clouds* (New York: Coward-McCann, 1961), pp. 95ff.

9. Daniel Berrigan, *No One Walks Waters* (New York: The Macmillan Co., 1966), p. 21.

10. Ibid.

11. Daniel Berrigan, *Love, Love at the End* (New York: The Macmillan Co., 1968), p. 94.

12. *Night Flight*, p. 49.

13. *Night Flight*, p. 135.

14. Daniel Berrigan and Thomas Lewis, *Trial Poems* (Boston: Beacon Press, 1970), "We sit or walk our cage."

15. Daniel Berrigan, "Life at the Edge," *The Christian Century*, 87:25 (June 24, 1970), 788–89.

16. *No One*, p. 41.

17. Ibid.

18. *Night Flight*, p. xviii.

19. *Night Flight*, p. 27.

20. Daniel Berrigan, *Consequences: Truth and. . . .* (New York: The Macmillan Co., 1966), p. 60.

21. *Night Flight*, p. 138.

22. Daniel Berrigan, *False Gods, Real Men* (New York: The Macmillan Co., 1969), p. 73.

23. Daniel Berrigan, *The Trial of the Catonsville Nine* (Boston: Beacon Press, 1970), p. 89.

24. *The Trial*, p. 94.

25. *Love*, p. 89.

26. *The Bow*, p. 146.

27. *Love*, p. 16.

28. Ibid.

29. *Love*, p. 9.

30. *Night Flight*, p. 5.

31. *The Bow*, p. 194.

32. *No One*, p. 48.

33. *No One*, p. 71.

34. *Night Flight*, p. 8.

35. *Love*, p. 98.

36. *No Bars*, p. 133.

37. *No Bars*, p. 134.

38. "Father Berrigan's Letter to the Weathermen," *The Village Voice,* January 21, 1971, p. 44.

39. Daniel Berrigan, *The Dark Night of Resistance* (New York: Doubleday & Co., 1971), p. 154.

40. *No Bars*, p. 58.

41. *The Trial*, p. 92.

42. *Consequences*, p. 17.

43. *Love*, p. 88.

44. *Love*, p. 95.

45. *No Bars*, p. 44.

Bibliography

Berrigan, Daniel. *Time Without Number*. New York: The Macmillan Co., 1957.

———. *The Bow in the Clouds*. New York: Coward-McCann, 1961.

———. *They Call Us Dead Men*. New York: The Macmillan Co., 1965.

———. *Consequences: Truth and. . . .* New York: The Macmillan Co., 1966.

———. *No One Walks Waters*. New York: The Macmillan Co., 1966.

———. *Love, Love at the End*. New York: The Macmillan Co., 1968.

———. *Night Flight to Hanoi*. New York: The Macmillan Co., 1968.

———. *False Gods, Real Men*. New York: The Macmillan Co., 1969.

Berrigan, Daniel and Lewis, Thomas. *Trial Poems.* Boston: The Beacon Press, 1970.

Berrigan, Daniel. *The Trial of the Catonsville Nine.* Boston: The Beacon Press, 1970.

——. *No Bars to Manhood.* New York: Doubleday & Co., 1970.

——. *The Dark Night of Resistance.* New York: Doubleday & Co., 1971.

Berrigan, Daniel and Coles, Robert. *The Geography of Faith.* Boston: The Beacon Press, 1971.

du Plessix Gray, Francine. *Divine Disobedience.* New York: Alfred A. Knopf, 1970.

Casey, William Van Etten and Nobile, Philip (eds.). *The Berrigans.* New York: Praeger, 1971.

IV - Malcolm X

In the seven years since his assassination, the impact of Malcolm X on America has greatly changed and expanded. Immediately following his murder, the news media portrayed him as a hateful and dangerous black racist. Now that perspective on his life and teaching has been gained through the social strife of the 1960s, he has emerged as a pivotal figure in the struggle for black liberation. Moreover, he has become a model of inspiration for militant whites who ally themselves with the liberation efforts of oppressed people. The religious experience of Malcolm X has usually been thought of in terms of his Muslim tenets. In this chapter I want to unfold a broader understanding of his religiousness. I explored the religious experiences of Guevara and Berrigan in terms of each man's life involvements. With Malcolm X it becomes especially important to connect his religiousness with distinct stages of his life. Any interpretation of the symbols of self-transcendence toward freedom in community must be placed in the context of the transformation of the man through three periods.

The first stage, of his early youth and young adulthood, was characterized by the enslavement of a criminal hustler to the destructive values of white America. The second period follows his prison experiences and conversion to the Nation of Islam. This was a time of racist separatism in which Malcolm X learned to cast out the "white devil" and gradually to discover his own manhood. The third phase occurred in his final year, when he broke with the Black Muslims, established his own Moslem Mosque, and traveled to Mecca. When assassins' bullets cut him down, the Malcolm of stage three had attained a remarkable degree of self-transcendence toward personal and communal freedom.

In the *Autobiography*, Malcolm X looks back on his early years as a time of personal dehumanization and degradation. He hated the white rapist's blood that flowed in his veins. He recalls with bitterness the terrible conditions of his father's death, which he believed was caused by whites who couldn't stand a self-respecting Negro. The indignities of the welfare system and the psychological deterioration of his mother pressed on the boy. He gradually learned what it meant to occupy a nigger's place in white society. Treated as a less than human mascot, he soon learned the vicious lesson of the ghetto that "everything in the world is a hustle."[1] Adolescence brought new experiences of self-depreciation so well exemplified in his painful attempts to "conk" his hair and in his abuse of Laura: "I was just deaf, blind and dumb."[2] As a black victim of the white man's social system, he turned to pimping, drug pushing, and the cocaine habit.

Yet, for all their destructiveness, these negative experiences of the young Malcolm were also the dark backdrop against which and because of which Malcolm, the later charismatic leader, could realize a remarkable height of self-transcendence. By experiencing the depths of human degradation, he was eventually disposed for radical self-transformations. But the early years also contain positive elements in the building of his character. He learned of the attempts of Marcus Garvey and others to better the lot of blacks; his stepsister, Ella, gave him his first experience of a proud black person. His boyhood in Boston taught him to avoid the superiority complex that certain blacks developed toward others; he would later disdain those of his own race who saw themselves as "house niggers" and not "field niggers."[3] Such "Toms" were all the more despicable pawns of the white oppressors. As the dapper Harlemite known as "Detroit Red," Malcolm sharpened his quick mind in the school of survival among the hustlers.

In an over-all estimate, however, the early years were irreligious not because Malcolm spurned churches and gained the nickname "Satan," but because of the stunting of his own growth toward freedom in community. During this period his inner symbols of coherence were those of the clever criminal on the make. He was limited to the hustler's pattern of meaning, namely, defining his manhood through the externals of money, pleasure, and power. Such a life produced a surface coherence that failed to cope with the deeper reaches of his own self-hatred. The motivating vision of the hustler further blocked authentic self-transcendence because of his pervasive lack of trust. The first rule was to trust no one outside his tight circle and to be slow to make intimates even of these. In such a perspective, the symbols of wonder were perverted by self-seeking and superficiality. His morality was less corrupted by reason of explicit criminal actions than because of the inner self-hatred and disrespect for others on which it was based. His sense of freedom at this time was a freedom from being caught and a license for self-indulgence. It was the freedom of a pusher who for the first time had some money in his pocket. This was a far cry from his later sense of freedom from self-despising and from external oppression, a freedom for a mutually respecting brotherhood. Without trust and living communication, genuine community was also impossible. His earliest years gave him little sense of human belonging in a wider community. He did find a certain warmth in the world of hustlers, but these glimpses of community were precarious and short-lived. Malcolm graphically depicted his own state of irreligion or inhumanity, his isolation from creative human relationships: "When you become an animal, a vulture in the ghetto as I had become, you enter a world of animals . . . it becomes truly the survival of the fittest."[4]

While he was serving a seven-year term in prison, the second phase of Malcolm X's life was launched by his intense conversion experience to the cause of the Nation of Islam. He had reached the bottom of a long downward spiral of degradation and self-depreciation. "The very enormity of my previous life's guilt prepared me to accept the truth."[5] It was at this point that he came upon the writings of Elijah Muhammad. Malcolm describes his prison *metanoia* in terms analogous to the conversion of St. Paul. Just as Paul was struck blind, every instinct of the ghetto jungle was struck numb in him. He described this experience as so difficult for him to undergo that it took him a week to get down on his knees to pray. Yet it was to become a change of heart that completely transformed his life. His account of this episode of finding Allah and Islam might have been copied from a classic hagiography:

> . . . swiftly my precious life's thinking pattern slid away from me, like snow off a roof. It is as though someone else I knew of had lived by hustling and crime. I would be startled to catch myself thinking in a remote way of my earlier self as another person.[6]

This moment of radical conversion was soon marked by a change of name; the hustler Malcolm Little became the crusading Black muslim, Malcolm X.

An important wonder aspect of the prison conversion was his almost blind loyalty and devotion to Elijah Muhammad, to whom Malcolm attributed his self-transcending salvation. It will later be necessary to investigate the role of Elijah as Saviour and Allah as God in the context of Malcolm's objective symbols of transcendence. Here I am mainly concerned with the inner experience of wonder that pervaded Malcolm at the sight of a letter or photograph of Elijah Muhammad. As the embodiment of the Nation of Islam, Elijah was at that point in Malcolm's life the symbol of a liberation from the living death of self-hating dehumanization. Malcolm says of his previous life: "throughout all this time . . . I was really dead—mentally dead. I just didn't know I was."[7] It was Muhammad who "virtually raised me from the dead."[8] As a part of this critical *metanoia,* the death/resurrection motif is a dominating theme.

Malcolm's conversion to the Nation of Islam provided him with a new symbol system for integrating his world view. The strange Black Muslim mythology of black superiority and goodness over against the oppressive perversity of the "white devil" supplied a mythological setting for the doctrine of black separation. Malcolm's new sense of coherence rested on the complete separation of twenty-two million ex-slaves from the white slave master and the return of these blacks to their own land. Because of his odd rendering of reality according to Yacub's History, Malcolm would spend twelve years as a Black Muslim making sweeping indictments of the entire white race.

A negative, futurist style of prophesying characterized Malcolm's outlook during most of his Black Muslim period. The evil world of white supremacy would be exposed and destroyed, and Mr. Muhammad was God's agent to effect this future upheaval. At the high point in his career as a Black Muslim leader, Malcolm expressed this perspective in a speech at Harvard: ". . . God has declared to Mr. Muhammad that the evil features of this wicked old world must be exposed, faced up to, and removed in order to make way for the new world which God himself is preparing to establish."[9] It was not enough to correct social injustices, as civil rights' advocates urged. For Malcolm, a radical day of reckoning, the time for a complete change, was at hand. His speeches during this phase manifest a number of qualities traditionally found in fervent evangelism. God, not man, would bring about a future, final reversal of the dominant order of things. "White America is doomed," Malcolm prophesied shortly after the assassination of John F. Kennedy; "death and devastating destruction hang at this very

moment in the skies over America."[10] The myopic vision of
the Nation of Islam served a twofold purpose in shaping a
coherent perspective for Malcolm X. Its symbolic language allowed him to conceptualize his ideas about the future in a way
that mitigated his frustration and despair over the plight of
black people in America. The Black Muslim symbolism also
helped him to understand the nature of white oppression in the
United States and to awaken the consciousness of other blacks to
their wretched state.

Although the negative, anti-white element prevailed in Malcolm's Muslim outlook, the Nation of Islam also held out a
positive way of life for its adherents. It offered a common
purpose and a hope of attaining a national home. It also gave
the believers an assurance of redemption in the present within
the Nation of Islam, separated from the corrupt world around
them. However irrational Yacub's History may appear to the
enlightened outsider, it supplied for Malcolm a set of theoretical
motivating symbols. The value of these energizing images lay not
in their logical or empirical validity, but rather in the perspective
they afforded on the basic black dilemma: ". . . blackness is
given a worthy status and the Negro heritage is made attractive."[11]

Malcolm's conviction that Islam as he then understood it was
the right religion for black people should be seen in contrast to his
views on Christianity. It was important that Malcolm deal
directly with Christianity, since so many fellow blacks had been
converted to it. While Islam was the "natural religion for the
black man,"[12] Christianity was the black man's curse. For it
taught the black, according to Malcolm, to hate his own black
humanity and love everything that was white. Christianity also
taught the black man to humbly accept his lowly condition,
to obey his masters, to sing and pray while always turning
the other cheek. It was a convenient religion for whites, who
could enjoy their heaven in this world, whereas blacks had
to wait for a hereafter. In brief, Christianity was incompatible
with the black man's hopes for human dignity and equality,

because its root doctrine of love was deformed: "Christian love is the white man's love for himself and his race."[13] By contrast, "For the man who is not white, Islam is the hope for justice and equality in the world we must build tomorrow."[14] Malcolm does not, however, apply his strictures against Christianity to the person of Jesus, who is also a prophetic figure in Islam. Jesus taught and lived a message of love, but this had been perverted by the white man. He believed in Christ, not in Christianity.

I have already noted Malcolm X's extraordinary experiences of wonder in his conversion to the Nation of Islam. In a more quiet but deeply felt key was his relationship to his wife, Betty. She was one of the few women that he trusted and the only woman that he ever even thought about loving. Malcolm speaks warmly of her devotion and understanding. In his profession of love for Betty, he goes beyond superficial views of love, which he claimed to be prevalent in Western civilization. In the latter perspective, when a woman loses her physical beauty, she loses her attraction. For Malcolm, Betty presented an unfading beauty, because her love transcended the physical. Her love was mainly a question of "disposition, behavior, attitude, thoughts, likes, dislikes—these things make a woman beautiful, a beautiful wife."[15] Later, in the trying days of his split with Elijah Muhammad, he depended heavily for strength from Betty, whose presence and depth of understanding comforted him.

The Nation of Islam also gave Malcolm a highly structured moral code, which provided a stabilizing ethic over against the loose life he had led. The fervent convert adhered diligently to the Spartan code of negative, individualistic morality, which has strong similarities to the ethic of sectarian holiness groups. His Muslim code was a litany of "no's": no dancing, no fornication, no tobacco, alcohol, or narcotics, no eating of pork, no gambling, movies, dating, long vacations, no lying or stealing or sleeping more than necessary. In his later years with the Black Muslims, Malcolm believed that this morality of individual asceticism should have been altered in the direction of concrete social involvements in the black man's over-all struggle for human rights. He gradually developed the insight that the Nation of Islam could be a more significant force for social change if it were engaged in actions for justice and equality in the wider American society. Malcolm's realization about the need for social activism eventually became an important reason for his break with the Nation of Islam.

A controversial aspect of Malcolm's moral orientation concerns the question of the use of violence for social change. Just as Malcolm was suspicious of Christian or Gandhian teaching that suggested a nonviolent approach, so he also swept aside Martin Luther King's dream of black and white together. He saw this dream as a nightmare by which the exploiting whites would continue to deny basic freedoms to the black man in America. He believed that a more militant posture than King's conciliating approach was needed. With an ironical twist, he claimed that Christianity's greatest miracle in America was that the black man had not become violent under white domination. Yet Malcolm's views on the use of violence must be placed within the context of his total strategy for the liberation of black people. He was dedicated to attaining the rights of the black man "by any means necessary." But this slogan ought not be misinterpreted. Malcolm X did not advocate violence for itself, but rather as a defense measure against the violence, hidden and overt, of the exploiting classes. He expressed this clearly on a number of occasions: ". . . it doesn't mean that I advocate violence, but at the same time I am not against using violence in self-defense. I don't even call it violence when it's self-defense, I call it intelligence."[16] Again, he maintained: "I believe it's a crime for anyone who is being brutalized to continue to accept that brutality without doing something to defend himself."[17]

It should be noted, however, that Malcolm's militancy underwent significant changes toward the end of his life. Before his falling out with Muhammad, his language about violence retained an apocalyptic and uncompromising tone. After the break with the Nation of Islam, Malcolm's prophetic stance shifts from that of rhetorical, doomsday preaching to that of the social activist who talks about violence in more practical terms. In his famous address "The Ballot or the Bullet" the question of using violence is dealt with in the light of historical circumstances as a measure of self-defense if certain social conditions and human rights are not realized. Moreover, the post-Mecca Malcolm would distinguish friends from enemies less according to color than according to their roles as exploiters or as allies. Thus, with these modifications, the directions and the quality of violence would also alter. In both the apocalyptic and the political stages of his understanding of violence, it was basically seen as a possible means for acquiring a greater measure of justice and humanity for black people.

The symbols of inner self-transcendence, during the second phase of his life, those of coherence, wonder, and morality, were moving Malcolm toward greater freedom and fuller community. After his conversion experience while still in prison, he exclaimed that he had never been so truly free. Malcolm's new-found freedom during this period can be equated to a new discovery of his inner worth. With the help of the racist doctrine, strict code, and exclusive society of the Black Muslims, he was able to transcend and reject the oppressive values of the white world that were at the foundation of his own self-hatred. Although the teachings of the Black Muslims appear fantastic, as I. F. Stone remarked: ". . . they are superbly suited to the task of shaking off the feeling of niggerness."[18] To be free from the stigma of "niggerness" meant for Malcolm a liberation from the psychological castration and dehumanization that American culture inflicts on talented black men. The Black Muslim experience freed him from the straitjacket of ·his previous history, but in a positive vein it also freed him for new modes of human relationship within the sectarian community of the Nation of Islam.

During the second phase of his life, Malcolm X's symbols of self-transcendence were fostered within the Black Muslim community. This communal experience consisted of a twofold rhythm of strict separation from the white devil and of engaging participation in the chosen black fellowship. Malcolm preached against both segregation and integration as these terms had been understood in the civil rights movement. Segregation meant that the white man would put the black ". . . away from him, but not far enough for you to be out of his jurisdiction."[19] Such segregation was a white method of controlling the life and liberty of blacks; segregation was forced by superiors on inferiors. Malcolm also opposed integration as a more subtle but effective means for keeping the black man in psychological and physical bondage. Integration was viewed as an attempt by white society to convert the blacks to a white value system that was inherently racist. Such integration would only succeed in increasing black self-hatred and alienation; through this process, blacks would never become masters of their own destinies. To overcome the fear, ignorance, and self-hatred inculcated by the white man, blacks had to group together into exclusive and separate communities. In these separate groups, blacks could learn a new self-confidence, self-respect, and self-sufficiency. Malcolm held that there could be no real equality and freedom for blacks until the blacks unified themselves into sustaining and militant communities.

He viewed integration as both "impossible and undesirable" and radical separation as a necessity. During most of his Black Muslim period, Malcolm's understanding of a separate black nation was influenced by the absolutist rhetoric of this religious sect. No compromise was possible; the pure, black race, led by God's emissary, Elijah Muhammad, wanted to separate itself physically and completely from the corruption of white society. Malcolm called for separate states or territories to be ceded to black people in America. His long-range program for blacks also included a return to their ancestral homeland, although his short-range program called for blacks to gain control of their own communities in this country. After his departure from the Nation of Islam, Malcolm would turn from the absolutist separation of the apocalyptic cult to a social-activist interpretation of separation for the goals of greater black unity and political effectiveness.

The second dimension of Malcolm X's sense of community during the Black Muslim period consisted of an enriching and fulfilling participation in the life of that exclusivist community. He experienced a deep sense of belonging among the brothers and sisters who loved their own blackness and respected their fellow blacks. It was for Malcolm a time of immersion in a new black self-transcendence through a community that enabled him to lift up his own sense of values. An example of these new values assimilated in the Black Muslim community was his transcendence of attachment to material possession that was so much a part of his hustler past. Whereas he would have once done anything for money, it had now become the last thing to cross his mind; his wife, Betty, attested to his continued freedom from materialist possessiveness. Even drug addicts could be welcomed into the community and made to feel for the first time the effects of black self-pride.

In contrast to the sham communication that existed between liberal whites and blacks, the Nation offered a place for frank exchange. By comparison with the downtrodden blacks who still lived in white-controlled ghettos or by contrast with the middle class, integrationist blacks "who can't get enough of nuzzling up to the white man,"[20] the Black Muslims made it possible for Malcolm to experience a community in which persons were truly respected as human beings. Although Malcolm was to undergo other important changes in his life process of self-transcendence, he would never forget the existential lessons learned in the community of the Nation of Islam: human rights and human respect. "That's what America's black masses want."[21]

The third stage of self-transcendence in the life of Malcolm X began with his traumatic break from the Black Muslim movement of Elijah Muhammad and culminated in his Mecca experience, in April 1964. Both of these high points in the development of his religiousness indicate an impressive ability to change and grow in keeping with his new insights. In his early years he demonstrated his willingness to learn from an experience and alter his outlook. When a teacher told him that being a lawyer was not a realistic goal for a nigger, ". . . it was then that I began to change—inside."[22] He later reflected on his degrading attempt to change his hair style to look more like a white person. Malcolm said of himself that his whole life had been a chronology of changes. A very knowledgeable commentator on Malcolm X has written: "One of the things that distinguished Malcolm from almost all his contemporaries was his ability to grow, to change, to move forward . . . to admit an error and correct it."[23] The religious experience, as an event of self-transcendence, calls for a willingness to risk a personal response to the invitation of a new set of circumstances and realizations. Without this disposition toward change, a person cannot break through to a fuller enhancement of his own freedom in community.

Malcolm X's split with Elijah Muhammad constituted a transition on a personal and theoretical level. There was the painful disillusionment with Muhammad, who had previously occupied the place of Malcolm's most significant model for imitation. The disclosure of Muhammad's betrayal of the Nation's principles by his own immorality, coupled with his growing suspicion about the popularity of Malcolm, forced the latter into another crucial *metanoia* situation. Although he submitted to being disciplined by Muhammad for statements about the Kennedy assassination, Malcolm was preparing to separate himself from the hierarchy of the black nationalist movement. The break also represented a shift in priorities from the mythological and apocalyptic orientation of an exclusivist cult to a direction of political action for concrete achievements in the wider black-liberation movement.

Well before the break with the Nation of Islam, Malcolm had expressed increasing concern about its lack of social action: "The messenger has seen God. He was with Allah and was given divine patience with the devil . . . the rest of us Black Muslims have not seen God, we don't have this gift of divine patience with the devil. The younger Black Muslims want to see some action."[24] His preaching about the great upheaval to be accomplished by Allah at some future date gave way to the teaching of social doctrines and current events to his younger followers. This movement from mythological prophecy to effective political power exemplifies an important aspect of revolutionary religiousness. Ideology, whether mythical or rational, assumes a secondary and ancillary relationship to the concrete, incarnate achievement of human liberation. Together with this movement from Muslim mythology to political action was a corresponding change within Malcolm from an exclusive to a more inclusive sense of fellowship. Political effectiveness in the black freedom struggle demanded some compromise and coalition with others who, though not of the intimate Mosque group, sympathized with its goals.

Malcolm's new goals were set forth in the Muslim Mosque, Inc., which he organized in New York City after the break with the Nation of Islam. This organization was dedicated to the elimination of political oppression, economic exploitation, and social degradation suffered by blacks. The mythology of Yacub's History had given way to a new set of motivational symbols. These images, while intensely anti-white racist, were enveloped with a revolutionary idiom that was well suited to the action orientation of young blacks. Malcolm's language during this time is heavy with Marxist overtones, although he never associated himself directly with Communist or socialist parties. Capitalism, with its hoarding of productive property and its domination by the wealthy few, is excoriated. Malcolm began to link "Dollarism" to racism in a systemic and not simply an individualistic way. During his last year, his travels abroad in pursuit of Afro-American solidarity deepened his consciousness of the international relationship between racism and other forms of economic and political exploitation. Part of Malcolm X's displeasure with the integration approach of civil rights leaders stemmed from his awareness of the tenacity and pervasiveness of world-wide structures of racist imperialism. The early civil rights advocates were deluded by optimism for rapid integration; the struggle against racism would demand a wider understanding and a stronger militancy.

He came to view Billy Graham evangelism, the subservient mass media, and the police, as the civilian army of the "haves." For Malcolm, this interrelated Establishment formed a carefully maintained network of forces for controlling and using the black man. At this stage of his development Malcolm's earlier detachment from personal possessions is refocused within a social context. With his "victim's-eye view" of the American dream, he tries to convince his black brothers that large amounts of American property should rightly belong to them but was unjustly withheld. For three centuries, he reminds them, their enslaved ancestors worked for no recompense; he urged the black man today to demand a just share of the ill-gotten wealth of white America. Malcolm X's growing socialist perspective during the period after his departure from the Nation represents a quest for symbols of wholeness on a personal and a communal plane. The coherence of his world view was altered to incorporate sociopolitical action in history as the road toward black liberation. His ethical outlook was also taking a new shape as he began to distinguish more diligently between individuals and groups on the basis of their exploitiveness rather than their race.

But this search for more adequate symbols of self-transcendence reaches a culminating point for Malcolm X during the final months of his life. What the establishment of the Moslem Mosque began, the pilgrimage to Mecca completed. As presented in the *Autobiography,* the Mecca experience was one of profound self-transcendence for Malcolm X. As his pilgrimage progresses, he attains new insight into the anti-racist dimensions of authentic Islam. He finds himself treated like a brother by blacks and whites alike; color finally ceases to be the sole determining element in separating devils from saints. His way of ordering the world has attained a new universalism. From the self-centered preoccupations of the hustler to the exclusivist and racist community of the Black Muslims, his perspective widens to include humanity as a whole:

> My thinking had been opened up wide in Mecca. In the long letters I wrote to friends, I tried to convey to them my new insights into the American black man's struggle and his problems, as well as the depths of my search for truth and justice.
> "I've had enough of someone else's propaganda," I had written to friends. I'm for the truth no matter who tells it. I'm a human being first and foremost and as such I am for whoever and whatever benefits humanity as a whole.[25]

Although Malcolm was deeply moved by the brotherhood he experienced on the pilgrimage, he was most likely aware of Arab and even African injustices to black people through slavery and other abuses.

As Malcolm X realizes in himself a wider perspective of the needs of humanity beyond the limitations of race, he transcends both his hustler and his Black Muslim self. He also rises to a fuller range of self-determination. The newly attained coherence permits neither the fatalism of the ghetto jungle existence nor the determinism of the Nation's apocalyptic mythology. He disclaims the propaganda that would deterministically prevent him from fashioning his own symbols for action in history. The sense of community involving all mankind is a positive symbol of coherence that brings together his previous interests in black solidarity through the Nation of Islam and his concern for militant political action toward freedom. A new master image is formed that can integrate black unity and worth with uncompromising political action and a surpassing sense of truth, justice, and brotherhood for humanity as a whole. Malcolm rose to a vision of a possible solution to racial hatred and oppression in the world brotherhood evidenced at Mecca, where people of all races could be one in worship. This experience allowed him to reappraise the white man, whom he had previously hated without distinction as the devil. Malcolm was able to differentiate for the first time between complexion and attitudes through his contacts with whites in the Holy Land. Conventional labels no longer determined his friends: ". . . some are even Uncle Toms! My friends today are black, brown, red, yellow and *white!*"[26]

The Mecca experience also represents a high point for observing the signs of wonder in Malcolm X's religiousness. He tells of being "utterly speechless and spellbound by the graciousness I see displayed all around me by people of all colors."[27] He was deeply moved by an almost physical feeling of love, humility, and brotherhood wherever he turned. The tangible experience of brotherhood caused him openly to exclaim his wonder at the power of God. Yet, in the midst of exaltation and celebration, Malcolm does not lose sight of historical reality; after the exclamation about brotherhood in the *Autobiography,* he gives a short talk about the inhumanity practiced on blacks in America. The last two years of his life were especially rich in experiences of wonder in positive and negative ways. As Malcolm followed his best convictions, he discovered a new joy of universal brotherhood and the happiness of a new mission to internationalize the black liberation struggle. Yet he also felt intense anger and disillusionment toward Elijah Muhammad as well as fear and anxiety about the safety of his own family. For the first time in his life he was shaping his own vision and conduct. Through the painful enterprise of transcending the Black Muslim philosophy and discipline, he rose to new levels of wonder in his self-knowledge and in his relations to others. The last chapters of the *Autobiography* ring with the voice of a man who suffered anguish and misunderstanding in his attempts ". . . to show a road to the salvation of America's very soul."[28] But Malcolm X knew from his own experiences the positive and negative poles in the dialectic of human wonder: ". . . it is only after the deepest darkness that the greatest joy can come. . . ."[29]

The last stage of his history also brought his ethical decision making to its fullest development. His new perception of brotherhood nuanced his judgments and conduct concerning the nature of racial injustice and the best ways to combat it. Freed from the interpretation of Yacub's History, he could grasp the social, psychological, and cultural roots of prejudice and discrimination. Because Malcolm chose not to alter his militant stance and language against racism in general, the American press failed to understand the important ethical modifications that had taken place in him during his final years. Popular magazines labeled him a violent demogogue at the time of his assassination.[30] Because he decided not to embrace the pacifist and conciliatory approach of the civil rights movement in the early 1960s, most observers gave scant attention to significant reformulations of his moral attitudes. The changes in his ethic of justice were matched by an ethic of love that now transcended racial and national limitations. It was not the love of a mild man but of an outspoken, active crusader for human rights. It was a militant love that sought political power in defense of freedom through uncompromising action.

The post-Black Muslim period also presents at its highest point of development Malcolm's attitude and decisions about death. From his boyhood days he openly confronted the possibility that he would die violently and that he should be prepared for it. This premonition of impending death stayed with him through his career of criminal activity. He believed that a man should live fully and then die violently; he would go to death-defying extremes to prove his bravery and leadership in the community of hustlers. In the second phase of his career, privately oriented bravado about death gives way to courage before death for the sake of a mission. After his prison conversion, he dedicates his whole life to telling the white man about his racism even though Malcolm had to die in the process. His loyalty to Muhammad was marked by a willingness to lay down his life for this master. As a Black Muslim preacher, Malcolm's confrontation with death takes on a new meaning and purpose. It becomes a risk to be incurred in order to build the Nation of Islam as a black state over against the white devil. Death ceases to be an individualistic consideration and is subordinated to the welfare of Elijah Muhammad's cult.

Indications of death are especially prevalent during his last year. He was constantly aware that a hired Negro, a white man, or a follower of Muhammad could kill him for a number of reasons. In this situation he realized that ". . . any moment of any day, or any night, could bring me death";[31] he did not expect to live long enough to read his autobiography in finished form. The premoniton of death continues, as does his courage in the face of a possibly violent end. But as Malcolm's self-understanding and vocation transcended the racism and restrictions of the middle period, so also his acceptance of death reflects a broader intentionality.

In the context of the world community of black solidarity and liberation that summons his final efforts, he sees his own demise as a risk supremely worth assuming. As the danger to his life greatly increased after the break with Muhammad, Malcolm's willingness to take risks also grew. Rather than withdraw from the public eye for his own protection, he multiplied his travels and speeches. He was so dedicated to the new vision of world brotherhood and solidarity for liberation that the imminence of death faded as a cause for fearful restraint. Two days before he was shot, he expressed his subordination of death to the cause of redeeming brotherhood:

> It is time for martyrs now. And if I am to be one, it will
> be in the cause of brotherhood. That's the only thing that
> can save this country. I've learned it the hard way—but
> I've learned it. And that's the significant thing.[32]

Each stage in Malcolm's life portrays his self-transcendence toward freedom in community. His three distinct and inter-related lives: Malcolm Little, Malcolm X, and El-Hajj Malik El-Shabazz manifest a progression in his inner motivating symbols toward freedom in community. He attempted to embody his third-phase vision of brotherhood and liberation by founding the Organization of Afro-American Unity. This move marked change in his conception of community from the narrow nationalism of the Black Muslims to the internationlism of the freedom movement of Third World peoples. He was able to combine the messianic fervor of the Nation of Islam with the political realism of his second period, while extending both orientations to comprehend a world-wide struggle for human rights. From this perspective he called on black people around the world to ". . . submerge our differences and create a unified black movement cutting across the U.S. and South America with deep roots in the African soil."[33]

Yet this black community, even as understood by Malcolm in his last days, was still a separatist movement. He never lost either his militancy, with its potential for violent means, nor his sense of black solidarity. What changed was the nature and goals of this black unity. It was no longer a separation based on racist doctrines of superiority over whites for the purpose of living apart from contaminating dialogue with any white person. But he never altered his belief in the necessity for oppressed blacks to organize their own liberation struggle; they had to build their own self-worth through a deep appreciation of black brotherhood and its self-determined endeavors for justice and equality. Thus his Organization for Afro-American Unity maintained the concept of black nationalism. It was no longer a territorial concept but rather one of ideological separation. And this separatism itself constituted a means for the personal and communal enhancement of blacks for the sake of the universal liberation of all oppressed people. It was a temporal separatism to be able to bring about an eventual unity of all races.

His Mecca experience gave him a new insight into the white man and how he could be integrated into the wider cause of brotherhood. Whereas whites were previously looked upon by Malcolm as devils who could do nothing for the black revolution, he later distinguished between exploitive and non-exploitive whites. The Malcolm of 1964 did not hate whites, but, rather, what whites had done to blacks. He was better able to understand the environment that nurtured white racism, while he would never justify or condone it. He came to realize that some whites were against racism, and he advocated a role for whites in the battle against this evil. Their function was to work against racism within the white community, the seedbed of America's racism. By working separately, sincere white and black people would actually be working together.

If Malcolm's final view of the internationalist black community was still a separatist conception, he did change his dire judgment of all white people; moreover, he invited them to take a crucial place in the liberation struggle. Perhaps Malcolm had a glimpse of a truly integrated future community when, a month before his death, he remarked to his biographer, Alex Haley, that he held racial intermarriage to be a question of personal choice. He also broadened his understanding of the role of woman in the revolution of the oppressed. After his second trip to Africa he spoke of the important place of women in the freedom struggle and of the need to foster the liberation of women. In a number of ways, therefore, Malcolm X was transcending the barriers of race and sex in his vision of the future community. Nevertheless, elements of separatism in Malcolm's understanding of black community were strategic factors for freeing the black man. Freedom by any means necessary implied the means of separation from the dominant culture. Malcolm knew that the black man had to take the initiative to free his inner self in order to become all that his potential would allow. If he wanted the white man to free him, the black would never be liberated from the old myths and ingrained perceptions about himself. Malcolm wanted to transform the passive civil rights movement into an active struggle for self-liberation and a consequent freedom in community.

The religious experience of Malcolm X manifests its subjective symbols of self-transcendence through the three stages of his life. The symbols of coherence, wonder, and morality that led to freedom in community assumed greater richness and depth as this black revolutionary pursued his own and his people's liberation. Yet a treatment of Malcolm X's religiousness would be incomplete without a consideration of the objective symbols of self-transcendence that acted as sources of power and attraction for his strivings. Two such objective symbols stand out in his life: Elijah Muhammad; and the Moslem term for deity, Allah. During his Black Muslim period, the historical symbol of a truly liberated black community was interpreted as a future reality to be effected mainly by Allah in his own time. Although Malcolm preached about the evil of the white man and his predicted destruction on some eschatological day, it was the life of the Nation of Islam as incarnated in the person of Elijah Muhammad that constituted the key objective symbol of self-transcendence for Malcolm during this period. Malcolm was caught up in the saving power of his semi-divine hero, Muhammad. He attested to having more faith in Elijah Muhammad than in any man on earth. He adored Muhammad as one who had the power of the sun, and he was committed to spreading Muhammad's teachings even at the cost of his life. During the early part of the split, Malcolm summed up his devotion to his master: "I am telling the truth. I loved the Nation and Mr. Muhammad. I lived for the Nation, and for Mr. Muhammad."[34]

It is understandable that such total devotion to a savior figure would have been an important facet of Malcolm's conversion from a self-centered ghetto hustler to an uncompromising Black Muslim minister. During the second phase of his career, Malcolm's extreme dedication to Mr. Muhammad was in itself a needed dimension of his personal self-transcendence beyond the stage of criminal existence. But the growth of Malcolm X's religious experience after the break with the Nation helped him to see that he had to transcend the security needs fulfilled in him by the divinization of Muhammad. In Mecca he realized that it was injurious to his spiritual development to make a deity of any man. "There on a Holy World hilltop, I realized how very dangerous it is for people to hold any human being in such esteem, especially to consider anyone some sort of 'directly guided' and 'protected' person."[35] Elijah Muhammad was no longer an objective symbol of divinity for Malcolm; his religious experience had evolved beyond such idolatry.

But Allah as an objective symbol of life and power, of ultimate cause and purpose, remains important in Malcolm's outlook to the very end. From the time of his conversion to the Nation of Islam, he explicitly referred to the power of Allah in his life. He had experienced the Islamic teaching that, if one takes one step toward Allah, he would take two steps toward the suppliant. Again, it was Allah who aided Malcolm ". . . to lift myself up from the muck and mire of this rotting world."[36] Yet to appreciate the function of the objective symbol of divinity in Malcolm's religious progress, we must explore the meaning with which Allah is invested in the last two phases of Malcolm's career. During the Black Muslim days, Allah is associated with the cult's doctrinal mythology. Allah is a deterministic divinity outside of history, who as an all-knowing and all-powerful ruler will impose his judgment on white devils by future intervention in history. "Allah" expresses a fatalism about the present and the future. Whoever goes against Allah's truth will be cursed in this life, and "everything is written" according to which the future is set.[37] Human effort to bring about change was very secondary. Malcolm's earlier years as a Muslim preacher show the results of such a religious perspective. His religiousness consisted in living the Nation's rules and preaching the Nation's futuristic mythology.

Yet even his Black Muslim days, taken as a whole, reflect a man who was in serious tension with this mythological and rigid conception of deity. As Malcolm came to identify with the political and cultural struggles for freedom of the black masses, the previous mythology about religion and God gave way to symbols of this-worldly religiousness. In opposition to the Nation's theology, he grew to believe that Allah was inclined to help those who helped themselves. Fatalism was being replaced by a conviction of self-determination in the changing of history. Although ahistorical doctrines of religion and deity were in evidence in his Black Muslim period, religion, in the sense of doctrine or of institutional structure, did not really dominate Malcolm's thought or activity. His ever-growing and chief concern was the freedom of black people through militant action. Allah and religion took on significance only in the context of the historical struggle: "I believe in a religion that believes in freedom. Any time I have to accept a religion that won't let me fight a battle for my people, I say to hell with that religion."[38]

In an over-all view of his religious development, Malcolm rejected a religion or deity enveloped in doctrinal myths removed from history, and he embraced as of overriding significance a religiousness of worldly ethics in history. His Moslem Mosque and OAAU were open to all blacks regardless of their religious belief or unbelief. What counted ultimately for Malcolm was human liberation; Allah and Islam made sense to him in as much as these symbols empowered the freedom movement. Through the struggles for justice and brotherhood for black people, he cultivated an attitude of respect and openness to the objectively transcendent. The Allah that he reverently refers to on the final page of the *Autobiography* has real meaning for him only in the context of eliminating "the racist cancer that is malignant in the body of America."[39] By following the religious experience of Malcolm X through its subjective and objective symbols of self-transcendence in the various stages of his life, I am compelled to conclude that he had achieved a remarkable synthesis of worldly religiousness. By the time the assassins' bullets felled him, Malcolm X had profoundly integrated within his revolutionary life a sense of history, myth, and religion. All these elements were embodied in a this-worldly purpose of living ". . . for whoever and whatever benefits humanity as a whole."[40]

Footnotes

1. Malcolm X, *The Autobiography of Malcolm X* (New York: Grove Press, 1966), p. 48.

2. *Autobiography*, p. 68.

3. Malcolm X, *Malcolm X Speaks*, ed. by George Breitman (New York: Grove Press, 1966), p. 10.

4. *Autobiography*, p. 102.

5. *Autobiography*, p. 163.

6. *Autobiography*, p. 170.

7. *Autobiography*, p. 125.

8. *Autobiography*, p. 296.

9. Archie Epps, ed., *The Speeches of Malcolm X at Harvard* (New York: William Morrow & Co., 1968), p. 117.

10. John H. Clarke, ed., *Malcolm X: the Man and His Times* (New York: Collier Books, 1969), p. 282.

11. E. U. Essien-Udom, *Black Nationalism: A Search for Identity in America* (New York: Dell Publishing Co., 1962), p. 142.

12. *Autobiography*, p. 155.

13. *Autobiography*, p. 237.

14. Ibid.

15. *Autobiography*, p. 232.

16. Clarke, p. 313.

17. *Autobiography*, p. 367.

18. I. F. Stone, "The Pilgrimage of Malcolm X," in *Black History: a Reappraisal*, ed. by Melvin Drimmer (New York: Doubleday & Co., 1968), p. 473.

19. *Malcolm X Speaks*, p. 42.

20. *Autobiography*, p. 272.

21. *Autobiography*, p. 272.

22. *Autobiography*, p. 37.

23. George Breitman and Albert Cleage, *Myths About Malcolm X* (New York: Merit Publishers, 1968), p. 15.

24. Epps, p. 32.

25. *Autobiography*, p. 366.

26. *Autobiography*, pp. 340, 375.

27. *Autobiography*, p. 339.

28. *Autobiography*, p. 377.

29. *Autobiography*, p. 379.

30. Malcolm foretold that the white press would identify him with hate at his death (*Autobiography*, p. 381). *Newsweek*'s story on his slaying depicted him as a weak desperado whose life was a series of provisional identities ("Death of a Desperado," *Newsweek*, March 8, 1965, p. 24). *Time* portrayed him as a purveyor of hatred and violence who obstructed the civil rights movement ("Death and Transfiguration," *Time*, March 5, 1965, pp. 23–25).

31. *Autobiography*, p. 378.

32. Clarke, p. 120.

33. Clarke, p. 117.

34. *Autobiography*, p. 292.

35. *Autobiography*, p. 365.

36. *Autobiography*, p. 287.

37. *Autobiography*, p. 149.

38. Malcolm X, *By Any Means Necessary*, ed. by George Breitman (New York: Pathfinder Press, 1970), p. 140.

39. *Autobiography*, p. 382.

40. *Autobiography*, p. 366.

Bibliography

Malcolm X. *The Autobiography of Malcolm X*. With the assistance of Alex Haley. New York: Grove Press, 1966.

———. *By Any Means Necessary*. Edited by George Breitman. New York: Pathfinder Press, 1970.

———. *Malcolm X Speaks*. Edited by George Breitman. New York: Grove Press, 1966.

———. *Malcolm X on Afro-American History*. New York: Merit Publishers, 1967.

———. *Malcolm X Talks to Young People*. New York: Merit Publishers, 1969.

Epps, Archie (ed.). *The Speeches of Malcolm X at Harvard*. New York: William Morrow & Co., 1968.

Breitman, George. *The Last Year of Malcolm X*. New York: Schocken Books, 1967.

Clarke, John Henrik (ed.). *Malcolm X: the Man and His Times*. New York: Collier Books, 1969.

Baldwin, James. *The Fire Next Time*. New York: Dial Press, 1963.

Clark, Kenneth B. (ed.). *The Negro Protest*. Boston: Beacon Press, 1963.

Cleaver, Eldridge. *Soul on Ice*. New York: McGraw-Hill, 1968.

Drimmer, Melvin (ed.). *Black History*. New York: Doubleday & Co., 1968.

Essien-Udom, E. U. *Black Nationalism: A Search for an Identity in America*. New York: Dell Publishing Co., 1962.

Jones, Le Roi. *Home: Social Essays*. New York: William Morrow & Co., 1966.

Lomax, Louis E. *When the Word Is Given*. Cleveland: World Publishing Co., 1963.

V - Martin Luther King, Jr.

In contrast to Malcolm X, the militant radical, Martin Luther King, Jr. represented the moderate militant. To the end of his life, Malcolm X was misunderstood and feared by most Americans. They were unwilling to face his unrelenting and scathing attack on white racism, his spirit of black separatism, and his talk about violence. In spite of the important developments in his life, Malcolm remained in the eyes of his countrymen the man from the ghetto: passionate, unpredictable, threatening. King, a middle-class black preacher with an excellent education, became this century's most respected Negro leader for great numbers of Americans. His personal charisms and courage, his nonviolent moderation, and the general sweep of his vision made him a unique mediative spokesman in the black freedom struggle. While important differences of theory and strategy remained to the end, the life experience of both men brought them to a similar form of militant yet reconciling religiousness.

Like Malcolm X, Martin King's religious experience was primarily a this-worldly journey of self-transcendence in the midst of political and legal efforts to free the black community from psychic and material slavery. Yet King, more than any of the other revolutionaries under study, spoke with explicit God language in the fervent evangelistic manner of a southern preacher. Much of his writing is steeped in Christian symbolism, which he employed effectively to inspire blacks and whites. There is no reason to deny King's adherence to such objective symbols of transcendence as Jesus, God, and church. These were important motivating images for him from his earliest years as the son of an Atlanta Baptist minister. I will argue that these symbols were secondary factors in his religious experience. His personal self-transcendence toward freedom in community was essentially a secular experience. After examining the chiefly this-worldly symbols of his openness to transcendent possibilities, we will be in a better position to explore the place of traditional Christian images in his religious experience.

A brief review of highlights in King's personal history will help to create a context for supporting the more abstract study of his subjective and objective symbols of self-transcendence. His intellectual journey manifested a movement from speculative to practical learning. During his theological formation, liberalism, with its confidence in human reason and man's abilities, challenged the fundamentalism of his early years. Yet it was the social ethics of Reinhold Niebuhr and European existentialism that began to give him a more realistic grasp of the concrete, historical situation. His study of Gandhi's doctrine on nonviolent resistance only became vital and personal for him in the specific episodes of the Montgomery bus boycott of the mid-1950s. King's speeches and writings reflect the educational heritage of Baptist piety, Niebuhrian ethics, Tillichian existentialism, and Gandhian nonviolence. But all this theoretical learning becomes relevant to his spirit and growth only when it is incorporated into painful decisions and risky actions. For King it was the anxious and dangerous days of the bus boycott in Montgomery that allowed him to experimentally link the spirit of the Sermon on the Mount to the method of Gandhi's nonviolent resistance.[1]

The movement in his life from traditional, institutional religion to a more worldly political involvement, a secular religiousness, can be noted in his statement of resignation from the pastorate of the Dexter Avenue Baptist Church, in 1960. His energies would henceforth be spent on concrete programs to eliminate discrimination and obtain civil rights for his people.[2] Although he continued to preach in his father's church in Atlanta, the pulpit became a secondary locus for his main concerns and messages. These were to be found in the streets and stores of southern towns, where the struggle for civil rights and integration was being waged. To discover the deepest religiousness of Martin King, it is necessary to explore the motivating images that gave him the courage to face beatings, night sticks, police dogs, fire hoses, and dingy city jails. His religious experience was intrinsically linked to the inspirational thoughts and the concrete involvements of his brief and significant history.

Birmingham and Selma were peak moments in the early 1960s for psychological and moral triumphs. The freedom rides, marches, and sit-ins awakened a new sense of self-esteem and a desire to organize among American blacks. These early civil rights actions also gave many liberal whites occasions to walk and suffer with their oppressed black countrymen. The early optimism of "black and white together" and the too-cheaply-bought assuagement of white liberal guilt would eventually be consumed in the flames of Watts, Detroit, and Newark. Yet the later struggles of black militancy and separation do not eliminate the significance of the nonviolent confrontations with the Bull Connors of Birmingham and the Jim Clarkes of Selma. These pages of American history would never have been written without the charismatic leadership of King. On the national level, the Washington March of 1963 was a culminating point of recognition for King's dream of a racially integrated nation. His winning of the Nobel Peace Prize in 1964 projected him into international prominence for his nonviolent approach to social change.

His history of self-transcending experiences also passed through the depressing periods of failure and disappointment. The civil rights campaign of Albany, Georgia and St. Augustine, Florida ended with meager results. Failures of tactics, of timing, of leadership, coupled with stiff opposition and legal maneuverings by the white establishment, conspired to thwart the aims of King's Southern Christian Leadership Conference. King's efforts in Chicago helped to strengthen SCLC's Operation Breadbasket, but Mayor Daley's powerful political machine and the strong ethnic prejudices of white groups blunted the effectiveness of King's endeavors. His leadership in the black community was especially threatened during the later 1960s by the rise of black power advocates and by disagreement with his anti-war activities.

The famous dialogue over black power between King and Stokely Carmichael during the Mississippi March of 1966 highlighted the growing rift among blacks between the civil rights moderates and the militant radicals. King continued to oppose the violent tendencies of the black liberation movement, but, in doing so, he risked the loss of many young people. They had become disillusioned and embittered by white intransigence and indifference to pleas for justice and brotherhood. Recourse to Marxist ideologies and violent strategies meant a rejection of King's middle-class faith in the ability of American institutions to be reformed from within. Martin King also came to understand the close link between economic poverty and political powerlessness for blacks, but he refused to accept violent approaches for resolving these problems. His final involvement, in the Memphis garbage strike, manifested his grasp of the relation between economic exploitation and racial oppression. But King was deeply distressed when younger blacks precipitated a riot during a Memphis march that he was leading.

A second challenge to his leadership arose from King's outspoken opposition to the American war in Vietnam. King spoke and demonstrated against the war long before such activity became popular. His interrelating of war and racism cost him the support of the Johnson administration, and it caused important differences with such moderate Negro leaders as Roy Wilkins and Bayard Rustin. They felt that King's international pronouncements were detracting from domestic efforts to achieve civil rights. King did not waver in his anti-war commitment, but, like the black power issue, the war question brought new difficulties to his plans for racial justice and new challenges to King's authority. It is important that our study of religious experience be kept within the broad historical canvas that has been sketched. For the inner history of Martin King and the objective symbols of his self-transcendence are intrinsically associated with the life events of the crusader for a nonviolent revolution in America.

The primary symbol of coherence by which Martin King ordered his life vision was that of a new interracial brotherhood. Against a background of American slavery and continued oppression of blacks, King was impelled by a vision of a new integration and transformation of society. To achieve this goal, profound changes would need to be realized in the national consciousness. King's inner perspective for meaning in life went beyond the concrete goals of achieving civil rights in matters of voting, schooling, jobs, housing, and other areas of political and cultural existence. All these elements were viewed as indispensable proximate steps on the road to the attainment of the new brotherhood; but the latter vision transcended any legal or political achievement. Brotherhood called for a new realization among blacks of their personal worth and dignity. King gave voice to this aspect of his ordering vision. ". . . with a spirit straining toward true self-esteem, the Negro must . . . say to himself and the world: 'I am somebody. I am a person. I am a man with dignity and honor. . . .' "[3]

Brotherhood also required the humanization of whites by the recognition and overcoming of their debasing prejudices in personal and social spheres. He maintained that redemption for whites and their elevation to new levels of brotherhood must be preceded by honest self-knowledge and acknowledgment of guilt. Just as the black man's oppression victimizes the white person in his humanity, so the Negro's liberation would enhance the humanity of whites. King thus summarized the overarching goal of his efforts: ". . . desegregation is only a partial, though necessary, step toward the final goal which we seek to realize, genuine intergroup and interpersonal living."[4] He spoke of this brotherhood as a vision of total interrelatedness. He understood that this vision of coherent and motivating power in him went beyond the seemingly possible and enforceable. This vision demanded that he and others commit themselves to "the perpetual doing of the impossible."[5] His vision of brotherhood required more than equitable laws; it called for an obedience to the unenforceable, that realm of inner attitudes and expressions that laws cannot regulate.

The enemy of King's coherent vision, therefore, is racism. Racist theory is based, for King, on a kind of dogmatic faith in the superiority of certain people over others. It leads to genocide of groups judged inferior because they are corrupt and defective, a constant threat to the superior group. This self-debasing contempt for life, as an unexamined dogmatic commitment, is a form of idolatry. Its genesis in America was closely related to the need to find a moral justification for a system of economic gain and political power. But gradually the idea of white supremacy was heightened and deepened in meaning and value so that it pointed beyond the historical structures of the relationships in which it emerged to human existence itself. King believed that this racist conviction supported the legal institution of slavery in the United States, underlay the Nazi conquests and atrocities in Europe, and fostered Western colonialism in the Third World. For King's fellow blacks the historical and philosophical dimensions of racism contributed to an inner pathology of self-depreciation and an external scourge of deprivation and suffering. Martin King's religious experience of self-transcendence was framed within the coherence symbols of brotherhood as a compelling goal and racism as the nemesis of the brotherhood vision.

Yet King's intellectual pattern of coherence was based in

large part on a prereflective optimism, a kind of primordial faith whose roots ultimately defy human analysis. At most, I can only point to some dimensions of this attitude of hope about a human situation plagued by apparently insurmountable obstacles. His optimism stemmed in part from a basic confidence in man's mental and moral ability to better social structures and to reverse his evil tendencies. His own tangible experiences of black people in America instilled in him a profound trust in their potential to survive in the face of wholesale exploitation and to rise above their deprivations to new levels of self-dignity and human achievement. Another source of this optimism was his own advantaged upbringing in a family of status and promise in the black community. This familial environment was again enhanced through the benefits of his own marriage and family life; King was a successful middle-class preacher and intellectual who saw the American system as reformable and promising, even for blacks.

These concrete experiences and encounters were probably more influential for building his optimistic faith in man than was his traditional religious background. His explicit faith in the benevolent and efficacious presence of divinity in the world was certainly not insignificant. But his Christian optimism itself was most likely conditioned very strongly by the existential experiences of prereflective faith fostered by his family and social milieu. Without the latter, the biblical optimism of his church-related preaching and life would have had little or no space to germinate and develop. The point at issue here is not that Martin King's explicit Christian faith was unimportant as a guiding force for his activities. Rather, I want to look beneath his Christianity to locate the human underpinnings of his assurance and optimism. The qualities of confidence and commitment in his own personality were nurtured and reinforced by the familial and class environment in which he was reared.

It is especially difficult to pinpoint those special moments of wonder in King's life that served as symbols of self-transcendent religiousness. There is no way of knowing whether the few examples singled out here were among the truly decisive symbols of wonder that acted as turning points in his life. Moreover, there may well have been unrecorded events that deeply influenced his affections: quiet moments with his wife[6] or perhaps a little-remembered sermon that could have been significant happenings in his dialectic of personal self-transcendence. Those familiar with the emotional intensity of King's oratory could with assurance cite certain peak incidents of his career such as the "I Have a Dream" speech at the 1963 Washington rally or his acceptance address on receiving the Nobel Prize as paramount moments of self-awakening and self-transcendence. The following random examples of moments of wonder in King's religious experience are in no sense complete or even adequate to account for the sense of awe in Martin King's life. These events simply indicate the genre of experiences that serve to illustrate a life of rich religious self-transcendence in and through secular involvements.

A moving experience for King was the scene in the Montgomery airport after the much publicized march from Selma. As he stood with supporters who were from different religious, occupational, racial, and educational backgrounds, he was affected by an inspiring vision: ". . . I was seeing a microcosm of the mankind of the future in this moment of luminous and genuine brotherhood."[7] He spoke of a culminating sense of awe when friends and events conspired to have him released from solitary confinement in Birmingham. He did not recall whether the sun was shining at that moment, but he knew that he could see bright light again. There were the supremely dramatic moments when Bull Connor's men were so touched by kneeling blacks that they refused to turn on their fire hoses. Again King was moved when his brother called to say that his home had been bombed, while in the background of the shattered house the singing of "We Shall Overcome" could be heard. King records: "I marveled that in a moment of such tragedy the Negro could still express himself with hope and with faith."[8]

Two final examples of moments of wonder emphasize the

close intermingling of the sacred and the secular in Martin King. When faced with the difficult decision in Birmingham of staying out of jail to raise bail funds for hundreds already incarcerated or of leading a forbidden march that would place him behind bars, King dramatically chose to head the march. He saw himself standing "at the center of all that my life had brought me,"[9] and around that center were his black associates of that evening and the twenty million black people who looked to the day of freedom from injustice. This moment of religious self-transcendence for King was nurtured and stimulated by the needs of his people. His symbols of wonder are intimately related to the secular struggles of the oppressed.

At an earlier phase of his career he spoke in more traditional religious language about such peak moments. During the Montgomery bus boycott he was terrified one night by threats against his life. He tells of sitting alone in the kitchen and of experiencing the presence of God, which reassured him to persevere. The context of this account is that of a sermon on God's help in time of need. Yet the situation in which he feels the wondrous experience is one immersed in a secular struggle for justice and equality in a southern city. Some of these examples of wonder reveal a combination of positive and negative dimensions, an intensity of exultation joined to experiences of pain and fear. These negative aspects will be further considered under the symbols of morality that concern suffering.

The keynote of King's inner symbols of moral motivation is a delicate interplay between justice and love. When these two dynamic elements energize ethical decisions, the new "colorless" brotherhood becomes a possibility. Echoes of Christian Neo-Realism can be heard in his attempts to fashion a creative synthesis of justice and love. Justice and love are indispensable correlatives for ethical decision and action: "Justice at its best is love correcting everything that stands against love."[10] King's involvements in the crucible of the civil rights struggle consumed any naive love ethic whereby appeals to individualistic benevolence were thought sufficient to achieve meaningful social reform. The professedly Christian rulers of Dixie and elsewhere were, as King well knew, only too anxious to hear the pious ethic of individual love that left unaltered social structures that favored the powerful and exploited the powerless. Thus, of necessity, the attainment of justice demanded a shifting of power from the haves to the have-nots. King had no illusions about the need for political and legal power in the pursuit of a liberating justice. Yet he maintained that power exercised for the sake of a more just order could easily lead to debasing hatreds by which both the victims and the victimizers would lose their humanity. Love for self and the other, especially for the enemy, was to King the chief humanizing sentiment: ". . . power without love is reckless and abusive and . . . love without power is sentimental and anemic."[11] He held that love was the only force capable of transforming an enemy into a friend.

Yet this ethic of love using power for obtaining justice needed a noble means for keeping all three elements in a creative and effective tension. King found this moral means in Christian and Gandhian teachings on nonviolence. Even before the method of direct nonviolent action became a lived reality for King, he came "to see for the first time that the Christian doctrine of love, operating through the Gandhian method of nonviolence, is one of the most potent weapons available to an oppressed people in their struggle for freedom."[12] Nonviolence meant not only the avoidance of physical violence, but also the elimination of the violence of the spirit. King urged the disciple of nonviolence not only to refuse to shoot an enemy, but to refuse to hate him as well. Non-co-operation in evil and direct nonviolent resistance are means in the Gandhian ethic, not ends; they aim at awakening in the victimizer a sense of shame and a renewal of his conscience from within.

The authentic proponent of nonviolence is intent on allowing his opponents to react humanly; by refusing a violent action, the satyagrahi does not permit his adversary to rationalize his own retaliating violence as self-defense. The true end of nonviolent action is the freely initiated, as opposed to the coerced, redemption of the opponent. It points to the reconciliation in brother-hood of persons who had previously been attackers and attacked. King held that the hoped-for aftermath of nonviolence is the creation of the beloved community, while the result of violence is tragic bitterness and recrimination. To achieve positive results through nonviolence required that the means used be as pure as the ends sought. King knew that it was not enough to rob an opponent of his moral conceit through nonviolent approaches; for he saw the actions of suffering love, demanded by the ethic of nonviolence, as life-enriching in themselves.

The modern champions of nonviolence have been clearly aware that such a life style requires a difficult change of heart in those who would practice it. Although King was dismayed by black violence in the last years of his life, he frequently marveled at the restraint and inner dignity of black Americans who disciplined themselves in the hard school of nonviolent action. The use of cattle prods and police dogs on long-suffering blacks was an indictment of the humanity of white society and a testimony to the humanity of those who might have been expected from their heritage of oppression to retaliate in kind. King stressed inner purification and transformation of attitudes and values in his disciples: ". . . non-violent soldiers are called upon to examine and burnish their greatest weapons—their heart, their conscience, their courage and their sense of justice."[13]

The many nonviolent confrontations from Montgomery to Memphis taught King that such actions for changing a basically violent status quo demanded deep self-possession and courage. He knew well that nonviolent tactics, whether of non-co-opera-tion or militant resistance, were not the recourse of cowards. For Martin King, "the beauty of non-violence is that in its own way and in its own time it seeks to break the chain reaction of evil."[14] In the same place, he spoke of the nonviolent method as a means of elevating the spirit of man. Thus King perceived the morality of nonviolence as an avenue of self-transcendence, as a way of going beyond the chain of violent stimulus and violent response, so typical of animal and human history. His commitment to nonviolence again portrays his optimism about humanity's ability to resolve its problems and ennoble its inner existence by the path of nonviolence.

Such idealism concerning the benefits of a nonviolent morality was matched in Martin King by a practical and political sense of its value. Commenting on the achievements of the summer civil rights campaign of 1963, he maintained that the practical result of the nonviolent approach was a confusion and paralysis of violent power structures against which the civil rights movement mobilized. King believed that restraint on the part of white police and other officials was due to the fact that black people consciously chose to protest peacefully. In those potentially explosive confrontations, nonviolence provided important psychological advantages for Negroes. It gave them a sense of new self-esteem in contrast to the white man's stereotypes of black people as irresponsible and aggression prone. The black man was able to feel in himself the dignity of struggle, of moral conviction, and of self-sacrifice for a noble cause. These practical gains for the blacks were also matched by winning legal and political victories against an adversary of superior physical force whose conscience was touched and whose arms were rendered less harmful by the nonviolent witness of the exploited.

King's assessment of the achievements of nonviolent resistance were later severely challenged by the rise of militant power groups. But the growing popularity among blacks of leaders such as Stokely Carmichael, Rap Brown, and Huey Newton forced King to re-examine and set forth with renewed vigor the practical benefits of nonviolence. In his analysis of the black power movement of the late sixties, King admitted to some values in the more militant stance, but he also saw grave difficulties in the idea of black power when compared with peaceful ways. He understood black power as an intensified cry of disappointment against American institutions which had betrayed and oppressed black people. It represented a deep frustration on the part of sensitive and intelligent younger blacks with the government's unfulfilled promises and its perverse set of priorities. It also represented a cry of disillusionment with the churches, black and white, and with middle-class liberals of both races. King saw nothing wrong with power in the pursuit of human rights, when that power was tempered by justice and love. For his own nonviolent method was also a form of power, which would enable blacks to determine their own destinies. King also realized that black power was a psychological call to manhood for blacks whose history had indoctrinated them to assume the role of "the perfect slave." For centuries the Negro was taught that he was a nobody. The black power movement was attempting to instill in the Negro a sense of his own worth, ". . . a deep feeling of racial pride and . . . an audacious appreciation of his heritage."[15]

But in an over-all estimate, King feared the negative aspects of the black power position. And in the end, his reasons for opposing the radical concept were more political and practical than philosophical. He viewed the black power ideology as a militaristic philosophy based on a sense of hopelessness about the Negro's chances to win his rights in America. Beneath his blackness, King was basically a middle-class libertarian who believed that the American system of legal, political, and social structures was fundamentally sound and could be made to work for the benefit of black people. Added to his appreciation of the American democratic heritage was an optimism about human potential for self-transcendence derived from both the Christian and the Gandhian traditions. He was chiefly disturbed about the despairing ethos of black power concerning American institutions. If blacks succumbed to the dominant mood of that movement, he thought, the realizable concrete goals of the civil rights struggle would be ignored, delayed, or suppressed.

King's practical orientation in the nonviolent approach is attested to by the reasons he gives to dissuade his people from jumping on the black power bandwagon. He was convinced that violent rebellion in this country would not work; it was doomed from the start, as were the slave revolts of Nat Turner and Denmark Vesey. He also argued that a violent revolution had no chance of success unless the revolutionary minority had widespread support among the nation's majority. He saw no such encouragement for violent revolution in the white majority. Moreover, a successful violent revolt demanded the allegiance and control of the armed forces; in America the police and the army were dominated by whites. Thus King termed the acts proposed by blacks who espoused violent overthrow as "blatantly illogical."[16] Again, practical considerations influenced his rejection of black separatism. Effectiveness in achieving concrete goals in a pluralistic society demanded that blacks form constructive alliances with other groups in the majority culture. He also recognized the need for blacks to organize themselves into forceful agencies for change, but he judged the separatism of the radical militants to be a disastrous dead end for the cause of black liberation.

It would be false to deny in King deep motivations for a nonviolent morality stemming from the beauty and excellence of such activity in itself for ennobling man. It always remained for him "the morally excellent way for the Negro to achieve freedom."[17] But his motivation for the nonviolent course was the pragmatic one of effectiveness in attaining specific ends for black Americans. His morality was mainly oriented toward practical actions: better salaries, voting rights, improved schools, job opportunities, and other specific action goals. King's symbols of morality reveal him to be a dedicated political man. He was not interested in heroes or histrionics unless he was convinced that they would lead to concrete ends. King's pragmatic and calculating secular morality, especially toward the end of his life, may be seen in clearer light by comparing it to the less pragmatic nonviolence of Berrigan. Berrigan's actions against government property were dramatic gestures geared to arouse a general awakening of the American conscience concerning the violent direction of its policies. Each of King's nonviolent direct actions had specific goals, usually in definite locations. It can be rightly maintained that Berrigan did not have to be so careful and calculating, because he did not represent a downtrodden minority group that had to move with special circumspection to wrest its just claims from a recalcitrant majority. Because of different social backgrounds, the nonviolent morality of these two men was variously nuanced. Berrigan's actions were those of a prophetic poet upholding moral principle, while King's nonviolent gestures were largely those of a political leader seeking definite purposes within the context of broader ethical concepts.

A morality of nonviolence in pursuit of concrete ends almost necessarily leads to actions of civil disobedience. Before the hatred and antipathy of an adversary could be transformed into constructive energy for social change, the latter must be placed in a position of creative tension. The community that constantly refused to negotiate must be forced to confront the issue. King did not perceive racial understanding as something to be created by or given to passive recipients; it was, rather, to be fashioned by well-planned actions over a long period. Civil disobedience therefore marked every step of King's civil rights struggles. He would first attempt to obtain legal permission for demonstrations, but when this was refused, the critical decision had to be reached whether to obey legal authorities or to transgress their mandates. King's judgments were always based on a careful weighing of the possibilities for concrete attainments and the value of appealing to a higher law or principle.

This ethical process can be noted from the time of the Montgomery bus boycott to King's projected poor peoples' march on Washington for the summer of 1968. The tentative steps of civil disobedience begun in Alabama would have culminated in the nation's capital as a massive civil disobedience strategy for social change. On the matter of civil disobedience a revealing comparison can be made between King, the pragmatic moralist, and Berrigan, the idealistic seer. From the Birmingham city jail, King appealed to a higher law to invalidate the unjust laws of segregationists, but he hastened to add that he did not advocate anarchy. He held that the person who broke the law should do so openly and with a willingness to pay the penalty. Here, again, King carefully assays the pragmatic consequences of his actions as an educational and apologetic move toward the black and the white communities. In the same famous message from Birmingham he adds another practical note to his action of civil disobedience: that his very staying in jail might arouse the consciences of the community over the injustice of the law.

Berrigan, on the other hand, refuses to submit to the penalty imposed by the court at Catonsville. He becomes a fugitive from the law to better demonstrate his contempt for the wider American system, which he sees involved in the greater evil and criminality of waging an unjust war. King's pragmatic civil disobedience maneuvers cautiously within the given system, whereas Berrigan risks the anarchy of flaunting the whole network of justice, which he sees as serving evil ends. Thus the violent means of coping with racial injustice was for King impractical as well as immoral. He clearly affirms its evil in principle: "Violence is immoral because it thrives on hatred rather than love."[18] But the main consideration for King's moral outlook is that nonviolent direct resistance represents a practically workable method of securing specific results for an oppressed minority amid a pluralistic and violent majority culture.

Yet it is precisely on the grounds of effectiveness that some critics have challenged Martin King's nonviolent approach. Louis Lomax cites King's Chicago campaign as a chief example of the impotence of the direct nonviolent method to change a highly complex socioeconomic metropolitan system. Chicago demonstrated, Lomax concluded, that an exploitive system would not yield its wealth and privilege to the nonviolent.[19] He saw black violence and black power as the principle means for future reform. Lomax, however, too quickly dismisses the power of nonviolence, even within a complicated economic and political area. King's Chicago efforts were too short-lived to render a judgment on them as drastic as Lomax's. Moreover, it is highly questionable from the present vantage point to say that black violence has been more effective for establishing black gains than has nonviolence.

Vincent Harding fashions a more subtle critique of King's

nonviolent style. He wonders whether a nonviolent movement can be authentic until the depressed people have at least been offered violent alternatives for reform.[20] Harding maintains that King may not have wanted to confront the necessary terror of efficacious violence. Others have cited King's bourgeois reflexes and Baptist conditioning as causal factors in curtailing his advocacy of the strongest power methods of realizing liberation goals. But it should be remembered that blacks have had the option to employ violence, especially in this century. It can be argued against Harding that precisely because King knew that blacks had this option and because he had looked hard at the disastrous prospects of its use that King pragmatically urged nonviolent resistance.

The interior symbols in King's religious experience of coherence, wonder, and morality must be placed into the context of a unifying and dynamic *metanoia*. King perceived life on all levels to be in a profound state of change. He saw himself as a nonviolent agent of that change. Man and society, in his view, were enveloped in a process of redemptive transition within the secular dimension of history. The dynamic process of change toward transcendent possibilities in this world implied a movement from old to new ways of thinking and experiencing for both persons and communities. For blacks this meant an inner change from self-hatred and its consequences to "develop a rugged sense of somebodyness."[21] For white Americans, the *metanoia* called for an acknowledgment of guilt for overt or latent racism, and a movement toward new forms of collaboration and fellowship with blacks. These interior changes were essential, disposing factors for a broader *metanoia* in the structures and ways of society. King's writings, especially during his final years, focus relentlessly on social change. When speaking of curing the cancerous forms of racism in the nation, he urged a radical restructuring of American society, a needed revolution of values and priorities in the land. He also repeatedly concentrated on concrete social changes in education, economics, politics, and other specific areas of national and international life.

King believed that the American black had a special role to perform in the process of social reform on a world-wide basis: ". . . the hope of the people of color in the world may well rest on the American Negro and his ability to reform the structures of racial imperialism from within and thusly turn the technology and wealth of the West to the task of liberating the world from want."[22] He envisions such *metanoia* on the scale of world history: "Humanity is waiting for something other than blind imitation of the past. . . . The world waits for this new kind of man and this new kind of power."[23] King's religious experience reveals a continuous process of change operating on the level of the human heart and consciousness, as well as on that of society at large. This *metanoia* is a worldly process by which individual and communal idolatries are unmasked for the sake of experiencing transcendent possibilities in human life.

King's experience of *metanoia* can be described in terms of a continuous dialectic of death and resurrection in a historical context. The moment of death is represented in the personal and communal suffering of King and those who would change the world according to his orientation. Suffering, not for itself but as a by-product of the struggle for a racially just society, becomes a privileged means for personal self-transcendence toward new realizations of value. The experience of suffering as an ennobling dimension of life has been consistently emphasized by King. In one of his earlier works, he spoke of transforming suffering into a creative force: ". . . I have attempted to see my personal ordeals as an opportunity to transfigure myself and heal the people involved in the tragic situation which now obtains."[24] This statement underscores the positive contribution that personal hardships made to his own sense of spiritual depth and vision. His sufferings also have the integrative effect of healing or making whole again a bitterly divided society. In his last full-length book, King reflects on the significance of the sufferings of the whole black community: "For us enduring the sacrifices of beatings, jailings, and even death . . . in removing a caste stigma . . . revolutionized our psychology and elevated the spiritual content of our being."[25] The theme of resurrection takes on profane connotations in his use of words such as "transfigure" and "elevate." It is a this-worldly transformation of minds, hearts, and institutions that he hoped would usher Americans into a new brotherhood.

By his attitude toward death King stressed the value of redemptive suffering as a vehicle for releasing persons from a death of the spirit to pursue the higher fellowship. Commenting on a threat against his life in St. Augustine, Florida, King enunciated his stance in the face of death: ". . . if physical death is the price that I must pay to free my white brother and all of my brothers and sisters from a permanent death of the spirit, then nothing can be more redemptive."[26] King then added a line from a Negro spiritual that spoke of going home to the Father to be saved. A literal interpretation of this lyric would conclude that resurrection for King pointed to life in another world. But a closer look at the motivating intention for facing death, that is, redemption from the slavery of racism for the sake of a new brotherhood, shows a this-worldly understanding of resurrection. There is no need to deny King's hope in life after death, but the real inspirational force for his willingness to confront death was an earthly vision of people freed from various forms of slavery.

The whole dynamic of Martin King's inner religious experience is directed toward the goal of freedom within human life. By freedom, King means the state of having options for self-determination, of being able to make self-initiated decisions for action, and the capacity to take responsibility for self and neighbor. He perceives freedom as the ability to deliberate, decide, and respond. King's complex conception of freedom must also be placed within the limits of both personal and historical destiny. Freedom is the chosen fulfillment of man's destined nature. Since man is defined as a finite freedom, anything that unjustly deprives him of human liberty is morally wrong, an abuse of man's nature. Racist segregation, therefore, as a form of psychic slavery and of external bondage, becomes for

King the paramount form of unfreedom. Freedom connotes a twofold movement: *from* the oppression of racism and *for* a brotherhood that respects the beauty of diversity. The positive direction of freedom for blacks requires a deep inner acceptance of their own worth, the development of that "rugged sense of somebodyness." Within the determinations of a given destiny, freedom did not entail for King an escape from history and its struggles. Rather, freedom had to be actively won within history by battling the forces of oppression.

King's experience of self-transcendence toward freedom can be realized only in community. Like the black separatists, he saw the imperative need for solidarity among blacks. He pleaded for group unity among his people; Negroes had to find greater solidarity and trust among themselves. But he knew that the oppressors wanted to weaken the potential for black rebellion by causing these declassed minorities to fight among themselves. Like Malcolm X, King's sense of community broadened in his later years to include the world community of all people of color. In contrast to the black separatists, however, King urged integrative alliances with the white community. He argued on pragmatic and philosophical grounds that there was no salvation for blacks in isolation. Blacks and whites were "bound together in a single garment of destiny."[27] King struggled against the growing tide of black separatism for the sake of a community in which "all life is interrelated."[28] There were no separate white and black paths to power and fulfillment. King's pragmatism and his spiritual optimism about mankind made him a mediator between blacks and whites in America; his tactics of nonviolent confrontation were always geared to fostering a reconciled community. The creation of tension through demonstrations, boycotts, and marches was a necessary preliminary for awakening adversaries to the prejudices and discriminations that impeded fuller community between them.

As King's leadership grew in the black liberation struggle, his sense of freedom in community expanded beyond the confines of the American racial situation. Or it would be more precise to say that he perceived more clearly the links between domestic racism and exploitation on the one hand and international issues on the other. He came to see that the downtrodden condition of the world's people of color could not be alleviated without a critical reform of international economic and political structures that contributed to the depressed existence of millions of men. The problems of racism ceased being merely questions of American history and became crucial issues of what he referred to as the "world house." He saw racism in the form of neo-colonialism, by which the life and destiny of whole nations were locked in the grasp of United States corporations. King spoke with new concern about the great majority of people in the world house who are ill-housed, undernourished, and subject to inhuman disabilities. He was able to place the poverty of the American Negro within the larger picture of world poverty. Within this wider context, he portrayed a special role for the American Negro, whose work was to reform the structures of racial imperialism from within "and thereby turn the technology and wealth of the West to the task of liberating the world from want."[29]

As King's experience of brotherhood expanded to embrace all underprivileged people, he also developed a more radical position on the nature and scope of the changes needed in America. He came to see that a reconstruction of the entire society and a revolution of values were required. As the momentum of the civil rights movement flagged in the late 1960s, he realized that American racism was more deeply embedded in the national character and institutions than he had previously believed. It was not simply a task of changing a few laws or dispelling a veneer of prejudice. The problem of racism was systemic; to combat it successfully, King grew to understand, the attack would have to be waged on a wide-ranging front. This could mean the nationalization of some industries, guaranteed incomes, and a vast review of domestic and foreign priorities. The freedom revolution of the world's people of color called for a profound transformation of priorities in our technological civilization, which in turn demanded a spiritual and moral re-awakening.

The enlargement of King's sense of community was particularly in evidence in his outspoken stand against the American involvement in Vietnam. The Johnson administration strongly resented King's anti-war stance and belittled it for lack of expert knowledge. Liberal blacks feared that King would stymie progress on civil rights matters at home by criticizing national policy in Asia. But King understood the far-reaching net of racism:

> . . . the cruel irony of watching Negro and white boys on TV screens as they kill and die together for a nation that has been unable to seat them together in the same schools. We watch them in brutal solidarity burning the huts of a poor village, but we realize that they could never live on the same block in Detroit.[30]

This statement shows King's perception of the racist dimensions of the war. Blacks are used to destroy poor Orientals for the benefit of white society. Again, as a national co-chairman of Clergy and Laity Concerned About Vietnam, King pinpointed the racial aspects of the war: "We are engaged in a war that seeks to turn the clock of history back and perpetuate white colonialism."[31] Like the revolutionary figures studied in previous chapters, King's experiences of self-transcendence toward freedom in community develop from a narrower sense of community to a wider one comprehending all mankind. Moreover, in the process of becoming more universal, King's religiousness also reflects more worldly concerns. The fundamentalist and abstract preoccupations of earlier stages of his religious development give way to a religiousness that is intimately related to issues of politics, economics, and social change.

In the perspective of this secular religiousness, King's objective symbols of self-transcendence are open to a worldly interpretation. As a committed churchman his external motivating images can be grouped under the traditionally religious words of "church" and "God." Church for King signified a community of followers of the gospel of Jesus; it was to be a fellowship of those who lived the morality of Jesus in the world. King understood the church as mainly an ethical community with this-worldly responsibilities concerning justice, love, and brotherhood. The church's failure to shoulder this moral commitment was a long-standing source of disappointment to him. In the days of slavery, organized religion was an accomplice of an evil status quo, using the Bible to bolster an inhuman system. From the Birmingham city jail he wrote that the church for the most part continued the pattern of ineffectual silence in the face of unjust laws. Of course, King loved the church as a nurturing environment for his own development and he appreciated the high points of suffering love in its history. It was these moments that he contrasted with the churches' present "social neglect and fear of being nonconformists."[32]

Two years after Birmingham, King reiterated his understanding of the church as an institution with high ethical goals but with deficient moral performances. Addressing the general synod of the United Church of Christ, he criticized the church: "In the midst of a nation rife with racial animosity, it too often has been content to mouth pious irrelevancies and sanctimonious trivialities. Called to combat social evils, it has often remained silent behind the anesthetizing security of stained-glass windows."[33] He went on to urge the church to move out into the arena of life, into areas of economic justice, housing, education, and police conduct. For King, the church has real meaning when it is involved in ethical issues, acting as a conscience for society and as an inspiring guide toward higher forms of brotherhood. The special role of the church is to "enkindle the imagination of mankind and fire the souls of men, imbuing them with . . . ardent love for truth and justice."[34] The church, therefore, operates as an important objective symbol of self-transcendence in King's religious experience. But it is basically a world-oriented image performing functions as a present and futurist symbol similar to the functions of Guevara's New People.

King's God belief and God language as objective images of self-transcendence present a seemingly inseparable challenge to my humanistic understanding of his religious experience. His sermons, speeches, and writings explicitly refer to God. He claims that the power of God was at work in his personal experiences of weakness and stength. When viewed in the wider perspective of King's life and works, however, the symbols of "God" and "religion" are essentially open-ended, humanistic, and immanent terms. The open-endedness of these images means that their power, significance, and reality transcend human control and explanation. When King uses these terms, he is pointing to the mystery of life that unfolds at the edges of human existence. In keeping with his Christian upbringing, he personifies this mystery, which can also be referred to as source, ground, the ultimate, or the unconditioned.

King wants to guard against a kind of idolatrous absolutism that deals with human existence and the cosmos in a way that would banish the symbols of mystery or transcendent power: "Any religion that is completely earthbound sells its birthright for a mess of naturalistic pottage. Religion, at its best, deals not only with man's preliminary concerns but with his inescapable ultimate concerns."[35] The same idea is personified in other places: "I am convinced that the universe is under the control of a loving purpose, and that in the struggle for righteousness, man has cosmic companionship."[36] In both these references, King declares his openness to a broader and empowering mystery. But this realm of ultimacy is intrinsic to, immanent to everyday life. For King, ". . . it is a living reality that has been validated in the experience of everyday life."[37]

It is precisely in his struggles for justice and brotherhood that the mystery of "God" or "religion" became profoundly real to him. Yet these words have for King a fundamentally this-worldly intentionality. God as the benevolent mystery of the universe is ultimately important for him as a force for bringing about a loving brotherhood among men. The principal intentionality of these transcendent symbols is humanistic and immanent. An example such as the following is typical of King's use of traditional symbols in thoroughly worldly ways: ". . . I thought of twenty million black people who dreamed that someday they might be able to cross the Red Sea of injustice and find their way to the promised land of integration."[38] In the last resort, King is concerned about man's earthly life first and foremost; his explicit openness to the realm of mystery and ultimacy, connoted by the word "God," is finally for the sake of creating a this-worldly brotherhood of love, peace, and justice.

The King legacy has come under renewed criticism in the past two years. His conciliatory approach toward the white establishment is judged as a compromise that bordered on the sellout.[39] In this estimate, he allowed himself to be manipulated by the power structure for its own advantage. He was intimidated, it is argued, by the threat of revealing his alleged sexual indiscretions and Communist associations. While it is true that King had a keen sense of possibly harmful publicity to his black liberation movement, there is scant hard evidence that he compromised basic principles. The final year of his life found him mounting his most powerful campaign to challenge the American power structure with a three-pronged attack on racism, militarism, and systemic poverty.

Others maintain that his moralistic, nonviolent tactics were too simplistically limited to confront the complex centers of economic and political power.[40] King's political theology did indeed entail the limitations of the nonviolent ethic. Such a stance called for an ability to alter strategy and to be satisfied at times with small gains. There is, moreover, abundant evidence to show that from 1965 to his death in 1968, Martin King was deeply conscious of political complexities that could not be dealt with by moralizing alone. Nor was King ever satisfied with appeals to conscientious principles; from Montgomery to Memphis he took the protests of the exploited to the streets in carefully calculated actions. But, in the end, he clung to the nonviolent ethic not because it was always a more effective way in the short run, but because it would eventually prove to be a superior road for the humanization of man.

Martin Luther King became in his own lifetime a symbol for self-transcendence to men of different races and nations. His martyr's death in the midst of the Memphis garbage strike fixed his image as unique leader in the black liberation movement. His human weaknesses, such as vanity and a certain pompousness, tended to recede, and the prophetic image of the nonviolent leader came to the fore as an empowering sign for others. He saw himself as a "transformed non-conformist," as a leader who had to stay a step ahead of popular consensus. The events of his life's journey helped him to spiritually transmute his non-conformity into creative direct nonviolent actions for social change. Yet he was always the mediating figure, occupying a center-left position among American reformers. He avoided the violent approach of the radical militants while moving beyond the more establishmentarian methods of traditional civil rights groups. He worked to instill a sense of "somebodyness" in fellow blacks, yet he rejected the separatist path to black liberation. He decried the evils of a white-dominated society, but he sought to aid whites to redeem themselves. King was essentially a loving critic of men and institutions; he fought racism but could not hate racists. As a dramatic embodiment of mediating non-conformity, he remains a very significant symbol for many who would struggle to transcend racism in themselves and their society toward a freer brotherhood. King's religious experience, therefore, continues to inspire the religious sojourn of others.

Footnotes

1. Martin Luther King, Jr., *Strength to Love* (New York: Pocket Books, 1964), p. 169.

2. Robert William Miller, *Martin Luther King, Jr.* (New York: Weybright & Talley, 1968), p. 85.

3. Martin Luther King, Jr., *Where Do We Go from Here* (New York: Bantam Books, 1968), pp. 50–51.

4. *Where*, p. 118.

5. *Where*, p. 142.

6. In *My Life with Martin Luther King, Jr.*, Coretta King records many moments of affective joy and emotional distress in her husband's life.

7. *Where*, p. 10.

8. Martin Luther King, Jr., *Why We Can't Wait* (New York: New American Library, 1964), p. 107.

9. *Why*, p. 72.

10. *Where*, p. 43.

11. *Where*, p. 69.

12. *Strength*, p. 169.

13. *Why*, p. 39.

14. *Where*, p. 72.

15. *Where*, p. 47.

16. *Where*, p. 67.

17. *Where*, p. 73.

18. Martin Luther King, Jr., *Stride Toward Freedom* (New York: Harper & Row, 1959), p. 213.

19. Louis E. Lomax, "When 'Nonviolence' Meets 'Black Power,'" in *Martin Luther King, Jr.: a Profile*, ed. by C. Lincoln (New York: Hill & Wang, 1970), p. 171.

20. Vincent Harding, "The Crisis of Powerless Morality," in Lincoln, *Martin Luther King, Jr.: a Profile*, p. 182.

21. *Where*, p. 144.

22. *Where*, p. 66.

23. *Where*, p. 77.

24. *Strength*, p. 172.

25. *Where*, pp. 102–3.

26. Miller, p. 189.

27. *Where*, p. 61.

28. *Where,* p. 211.

29. *Where,* p. 66.

30. Martin Luther King, Jr., *The Trumpet of Conscience* (New York: Harper & Row, 1968), p. 23.

31. Martin Luther King, Jr., et al., *Speech on the War in Vietnam* (New York: Clergy and Laity Concerned About Vietnam, 1967), p. 6.

32. *Why,* p. 91.

33. Miller, p. 226.

34. Miller, p. 227.

35. Martin Luther King, Jr., *I Have a Dream,* edited by Lotte Hoskins (New York: Grosset & Dunlap, 1968), p. 117.

36. *I Have,* p. 47.

37. *I Have,* p. 48.

38. *Why,* p. 73.

39. This is a major theme in John Williams, *The King God Didn't Save* (New York: Coward-McCann, 1970).

40. David L. Lewis, *King: A Critical Biography* (New York: Praeger, 1970) summarizes in his concluding chapter the limitations of King's nonviolent approach. Hanes Walton, *The Political Philosophy of Martin Luther King, Jr.* (Westport, Conn.: Greenwood Publishing Corp., 1971) criticizes King's univocal, moral method for failing to come to grips with political plurality and complexity.

Bibliography

King, Martin Luther, Jr. *Stride Toward Freedom.* New York: Harper & Row, 1959.

————. *The Measure of a Man.* Philadelphia: United Church Press, 1959.

————. *Why We Can't Wait.* New York: New American Library, 1964.

————. *Strength To Love.* New York: Pocket Books, 1964.

————. *Where Do We Go from Here: Chaos or Community?* New York: Bantam Books, 1968.

————. *The Trumpet of Conscience.* New York: Harper & Row, 1968.

————. *I Have a Dream.* Edited by Lotte Hoskins. New York: Grosset & Dunlap, 1968.

Bennett, Lerone, Jr. *What Manner of Man.* New York: Pocket Books, 1965.

King, Coretta Scott. *My Life with Martin Luther King, Jr.* New York: Holt, Rinehart & Winston, 1969.

Lewis, David L. *King: A Critical Biography.* New York: Praeger, 1970.

Lincoln, C. Eric (ed.). *Martin Luther King, Jr.: a Profile*. New York: Hill & Wang, 1970.

Lokos, Lionel. *House Divided: the Life and Legacy of Martin Luther King*. New York: Arlington House, 1968.

Lomax, Louis E. *To Kill a Black Man*. Los Angeles: Holloway House Publishing Co., 1968.

Miller, Robert William. *Martin Luther King, Jr.* New York: Weybright & Talley, 1968.

Walton, Hanes. *The Political Philosophy of Martin Luther King, Jr.* Westport, Conn.: Greenwood Publishing Corp., 1971.

Williams, John. *The King God Didn't Save*. New York: Coward-McCann, 1970.

Two different views on King's assassination:

Huie, William Bradford. *He Slew the Dreamer*. New York: Delacorte Press, 1970.

Weisberg, Harold. *Frame-Up: The Martin Luther King/James Earl Ray Case*. New York: Outerbridge & Dienstfrey/Dutton, 1971.

VI - Abbie Hoffman

Of all the radical figures studied in this book, Abbie Hoffman would seem to be the most unlikely candidate either as a revolutionary or as a religionist. He is not an international hero, like Guevara and Fanon, both leaders and spokesmen for great revolutionary movements. Nor is Hoffman a national reformer of the stature of King and Malcolm X. Traditional religion is rarely to be found in his writings except as the butt of his satirical humor. Yet Hoffman represents a significant form of revolutionary religiousness when his activities and thought are examined in the light of the model for exploration. As a prophetic jester he ridicules the conventional myths and rituals by which America lives. His outlandish antics and biting mockery threaten the national ethos and self-confidence more deeply than orderly rallies and marches. This is especially true for a sizable portion of the young, whose disillusionment with time-honored institutions he reflects. Moreover, Hoffman portrays an important kind of "Yippie" religiousness, the unusual mode of self-transcendence of this cultural revolutionary.

Hoffman's life has been characterized at every step by a

spirit of rebellious non-conformity joined to concern for social reform. After expulsion from public school and a stint at hustling pool, he made his way to Brandeis University, where he was exposed to such thinkers as Herbert Marcuse and Abraham Maslow. He became active in civil rights groups in New England, and in the mid-sixties worked in various southern political and educational projects for black people. Yet involvement in the social crusades of the early years of the 1960s taught persons such as Hoffman that the American economic and political system was not easily amenable to change by working through given channels. The hippie counterculture was beginning to move East from San Francisco in late 1966. Abbie saw in the hippie culture a potent means for a cultural change in America that would eventually alter the nation's commitments more profoundly than the traditional civil rights and New Left political movements. The latter could effect certain legal changes within the system, but the hippie phenomenon represented for Hoffman a more radical way of changing basic attitudes and priorities among Americans.

His own rational bent and quixotic enthusiasms gave rise to the Yippie wing (Youth International Party) of the cultural revolution, whose characteristics will be the major focus of this chapter. Hoffman sees himself as a cultural revolutionary, as distinct from a political revolutionary. The latter, according to Abbie, strives to change other people and institutions, whereas cultural revolution requires that people change their own way of living and acting.[1] The cultural revolution goes beyond political change, because it seeks to alter the total context of sensitivities and assumptions in which political choice and action take place. The cultural revolution produces psychic as well as physical liberation. But a closer examination of the Yippie dimensions of the cultural revolution manifests Hoffman's continuing commitment to political renewal as well. His Yippie antics are eminently political, as opposed to the individualistic or communal withdrawal from "straight" society of other hippie groups. Hoffman wants to combine politics and art, Fidel Castro's passion for social change with Andy Warhol's use of the modern media. He is a political hippie.

As an originator of the Yippie movement, therefore, Hoffman represents a blending of certain hippie qualities with New Left political concerns. Although he can be severely critical of the ideological "ego trips" of political reformers, the Yippie wants to promote communication among the different factions of the counterculture for the ultimate goal of fundamental political-cultural reform. But as a Yippie revolutionary, Hoffman wants to go beyond theorizing and conventional politicking to dramatizing in his present life style the attitudes and actions of the alternative society he seeks to establish. While he is not opposed to violence as self-defense or even as a visible means to put down oppression, he is realistic enough to know that neither violent confrontation nor hippie withdrawal will work to change the American system. In keeping with his own imaginative talents and predilections, he has done much to devise a potent and acceptable method for social change, that of revolutionary-action theater. By the creation of dramatic myths and the manipulation of mass media, the Yippie is at once a trenchant satirist of the dominant culture and an educator through his own life style toward an alternative social reality. Exaggeration in word and action is part of the dramatic statement that can jolt people loose from the familiar enslavements of their daily lives and expand their consciousness of alternate ways of living. Thus all of Hoffman's modes of ridiculing, "fucking," and "ripping off" the system must be understood as an essentially serious and earnest endeavor to transcend the structures, mores, and mentalities of what he sees as an oppressive sociocultural environment.

We can best understand the religious experience of Abbie Hoffman by focusing on the central element of the revolutionary self-transcendence involved in going from Pig Nation to Woodstock Nation. Although these terms intersect with concrete places, persons, and events, they are mainly states of mind and styles of life. A revolution of values and commitments is required to journey from *Amerika* to the America of Hoffman's vision. The former is the all too prevalent land of vicious competition, authoritarian control over others, exploitation of nature, and thralldom to money, plastic pleasure, and prestige. The positive ideal of Hoffman's America comes through as a network of human relationships in which co-operation, autonomy, the pleasures of nature, and man are uppermost. Thus the religious experience of Hoffman must be placed in the context of transcending a chaotic and destructive consciousness and society in the search for a human existence in which nature, the self, and the other can interrelate in creativity and joy. His religiousness is to be found in the revolutionary struggle to effect such a change according to Yippie tactics. Hoffman's symbols of coherence all point to this central experience of revolutionary transcendence from a present social and psychic order of deadly oppression for man to a new order of brotherhood and self-fulfillment. His motivating symbols of morality, of judging good and evil, cluster around the same paradigm. This cultural revolution is also the locus of his experiences of wonder in positive and negative ways.

The religiousness of Abbie Hoffman consists in a kind of inner *metanoia,* a revolution of mind and heart that will have as a by-product a revolution of social and political structures. Institutional change is secondary to the alteration of man's consciousness. He quotes Cohn-Bendit that "the real meaning of revolution is not change in management but a change in man."[2] This *metanoia* necessitates the purposeful choosing of a new way of living in the present. Each individual must take the step by himself for himself. The religion of Hoffman is a "head revolution"; he talks about blowing people's minds, which in the language of Charles Reich's Consciousness III means a revolution in human awareness:

> It [Consciousness III] is most important because its aim is nothing less than to restore man's awareness of himself, of other people, of nature, of his own life. It seeks to make

man, in everything that he does or experiences, more alive.
To "blow one's mind" means to become more aware.[3]

The alienation to be overcome through the cultural revolution is primarily psychic; class and racial factors of this alienation are symptoms of a deeper estrangement rooted inside each man. This is why Abbie tells his followers not to fit into existing movements and fulfill others' expectations, but rather to "organize your head," and create their own non-alienating inner revolution. "Don't organize students, teachers, Negroes, organize your head. Find out where you are, what you want to do and go out and do it."[4] In brief, the Yippie revolution is a kind of second birth, which demands a death to the value scheme of Pig Nation. In this connotation, Hoffman favorably cites Bob Dylan: "He not busy being born, is busy dying."[5] It is a revolution for everyone, because it seeks to transform one's deepest sense of self. Hoffman wants to liberate capitalists, Communists, rich and poor, young and old. In the words of Jerry Rubin: "Yippies believe every nonyippie is a repressed yippie. We try to bring out the yippie in everybody."[6]

To better appreciate the means and intrinsically related goals of Yippie self-transcendence, it would be helpful to portray in broad strokes the lineaments of Pig Nation as seen by Hoffman. Exaggeration is an important part of his style; his caricatures of *Amerika* became the theatrical props of overstatement for impressing his point on an audience. Hoffman sees the technocratic society in which he grew up as a corporate state aimed at controlling and manipulating persons. Life is highly scheduled and determined to the end of maximizing profits and production regardless of cost to human growth and dignity. Suppression of inner needs and conformity to alien standards are the ways to success. Status is measured by affluence. Discipline and self-denial are key virtues that permit a man to achieve his acquisitive goals in a social order based on competition. Hoffman sees *Amerika* as a land that embraced the philosophy of the survival of the fittest or of the most ruthless. Life is approached with a law-and-order mentality; renunciation of instinct is essential to a civilization that defines itself according to efficient productivity. When greed, aggression, and jealousy interfere with the smooth functioning of the productive apparatus, they must be rigidly controlled. When the same qualities operate to foster productivity, they are prized as the noble civic virtues of ambition, drive, and the desire for self-advancement.

In Pig Nation, technocracy places rationality, objectivity, and calculation over aesthetic and sensual pleasures. Technical experts rise to the top of the social pecking order, as they alone are deemed capable of providing insights and answers to life's problems, always in keeping with the criterion of material productivity. In this system educational degrees and level of income indicate a man's level of importance within society. "Having arrived" is calculated by the accumulation of material goods. Racism and economic exploitation of minorities and the poor are indispensable elements of domestic policy in the *Amerika* that exists to benefit its technocratic elite and their political and financial managers. Militarism and the bloody domination of foreign peoples are natural extensions of Pig Nation's rapacious need to feed the voracious appetites of its production machine and protect its markets abroad.

Such a rigid hierarchy of externally oriented goals destroys the potential for a feeling of authentic community. Frustration, powerlessness, and guilt eventually characterize *Amerika*'s relentless pursuit. Such, in broad strokes, is the picture of the technocratic society that Hoffman seeks to transcend. It is easy enough to criticize his simplistic black and white portrayal of the American scene. But exaggerations are the interpretative tools of the prophetic jester; careful distinctions and qualifications are the nemesis of the kind of psychic awakening that Hoffman wants to produce in people who all too readily blind themselves to the evils of their society in order to enjoy its fruits without being challenged in mind and conscience. Others may argue that Hoffman's exaggerations will repel the very people he wants to convert. To this objection, Hoffman would reply that the Yippie doesn't care about swaying others; he is busy "doing his own thing," which requires a brutally frank gaze at the conditioning of Pig *Amerika*. Moreover, there is good reason to believe that many younger persons are influenced by the methods and message of the Yippie dramatists.

The religious self-transcendence of Pig Nation for Hoffman consists in living out the contrasting virtues of Woodstock Nation. Again, this is a psychic state, a zone of inner liberation that inspires the non-conformist conduct of the Yippie. Liberation from the constrictive bonds of Pig Nation is an underlying principle of his religiousness. But his idea of liberating self-transcendence is also a positive "freedom for," as is well expressed by Reich:

> The foundation for Consciousness III [we can substitute Woodstock Nation] is liberation. It comes into being the moment the individual frees himself from automatic acceptance of the imperatives of society and the false consciousness which society imposes . . . the meaning of liberation is that the individual is free to build his own philosophy and values, his own life-style, and his own culture from a new beginning.[7]

In Hoffman's less academic words, he speaks of himself as a cultural revolutionary "concerned with building and defending the new NATION that gave us a glimpse of its beauty on the shores of White Lake in the Catskill Mountains."[8] He is dedicated to creating "liberated land in which we can do whatever the fuck we decide." And he sees himself "guilty of helping to bring Woodstock Nation to the whole earth."[9] The religiousness of Abbie Hoffman, therefore, can be aptly expressed as the pursuit of freedom, as a struggle for liberation from an oppressive society and a stifled selfhood toward a richer and more authentic commitment to self and others.

To appreciate the religiousness of Woodstock Nation, it is important to understand that it is not a religion of doctrinal beliefs or ethical codes. It is a life style that embodies a creed, code, and cult in the very actions of living it out. In the language of another Yippie spokesman, religion is "what you do all day, how you live."[10] It is openness to people, ideas, feelings, nature—to all possibilities for transcendent experiences. In the Yippie mode, this religious action can have to do with long hair, frisbees, clouds, waves, somersaults, and sunrises. It can pertain to any form of human liberation, or making life a "groovy trip." It means the freedom to do, to be, to decide and undecide. The religion of Yippiehood is a matter of "turning on" to life and all its potential. The goals of Yippie religiousness cannot be separated from the concrete means by which it is expressed. Thus by studying the main methods for manifesting and communicating Hoffman's style of self-transcendence, the religiousness of Woodstock Nation over against Pig Nation will be revealed.

Theatrical creation and performance of new myths is an important road for self-transcendence in Woodstock Nation. The Yippie myth, whether that of levitating the Pentagon or seeing the 1968 Democratic Convention in Chicago as a Festival of Life, is a way of inviting people to participate in alternative modes of consciousness as the first step toward an alternative society. In the spirit of Artaud's Theater of Cruelty, Hoffman wants "to address the entire organism through an intensive mobilization of objects, gestures and signs . . . to restore a passionate . . . conception of life."[11] Such dramatic presentations must have the possibilities of direct participation, like his own Yippie wedding in Central Park or the episode of throwing away money at the New York Stock Exchange. The dramatic statement should also have an element of mystery, confusion, and even contradiction. Symbolic action itself is richer in meaning than rational explanations that abstract from the complexity of the concrete gesture. Some confusion and contradiction are necessary to disengage people from conventional wisdom and familiar but unquestioned conduct. "Confusion is mightier than the sword,"[12] says Hoffman in reference to his theater of the streets.

In order to "dynamite brain cells" and be "putting people through changes,"[13] it is vital to explode the accepted assurances of people in the bureaucratic clarity and predictability of Pig Nation. A role of dramatic mythmaking consists in the shattering of fixed categories in order that new possibilities may be perceived. Moreover, the fashioning of odd and ever new myths permits Yippies to avoid self-definition. They thus preserve the freedom to become whatever "will fuck the system." An absurdly comic gesture such as wearing a Revolutionary War uniform to a hearing of a Congressional investigating committee dramatizes both the ridiculous seriousness of the hearing and its departure from the libertarian heritage of the founding fathers. Hoffman, incidentally, finds power in certain myths of early America which he believes subsequent institutions have warped. Against the programmed dullness of the corporate state, Yippie theater urges spontaneity. Pig Nation cannot trust men; the spontaneity of Yippie drama implies a trust of one's organism and its impulses. Bizarre costumes and other unusual props broadcast the Yippie vision of a new form of community. Hoffman distinguishes between uniforms and costumes. Uniforms connote the conformity and restrictions imposed on man's creative spirit by the present ruling order; costumes express diversity and free choice.

Dramatic expression for Hoffman is an avenue toward greater freedom and self-transcendence. By following his creative and comic imagination, he acts in ways that help him ascend to new levels of self-realization and open up unsuspected horizons for others caught in the treadmill existence of *Amerika*. He understands that drama is an ancient and powerful expression of populist feelings and needs. Hoffman knows that if he can appeal to these rudimentary instincts of popular fantasy and mysticism, he will have devised an instrument for social change more forceful than reasoned essays and political speeches. Guerrilla theater awakens in the popular subconscious through

comic satire and stimulating fantasies a whole range of possibilities for altering society and the self. Drama, therefore, as a
means of Yippie self-transcendence is at the core of this important political and cultural development, which has a number
of counterparts in college groups and mime troupes across the
land.

Hoffman accounts for his movement in terms of drama: "We
are theatre in the streets, total and committed . . . the aim is to
get people to do, to participate, whether positively or negatively."[14] Dramatic participation is a kind of liturgical act, a
sacramental sharing that is usually more intense and engaging
for the whole person than traditional religious rituals. He en-
titles a chapter on the 1968 Democratic Convention in theatrical
terms: "Chicago: Festival of Life. Produced by Marshall
McLuhan. Directed by Mayor Daley and Antonin Artaud."
Jerry Rubin's Yippie manifesto, Do It!, is subtitled "Scenarios
of the Revolution." Hoffman also possesses a keen sense of how
best to exploit the mass media in presenting his theater. He
found that if the Yippies created a "mind-blowing" scene
through street theater, love-ins, and other happenings, the news
media would invariably distort and expand the incident, creating a new myth in the process. Television and newspapers would
thereby become unwitting accomplices of Yippie purposes by
projecting the fantasy/myth far and wide into the consciousness
of American society.

Closely related to the dramatic route to self-transcendence in
Hoffman's perspective is his cultivation of a Dionysian life style.
Drama itself was developed in ancient Greece as a religious
festival honoring Dionysus. Hoffman wants to transcend the
dominant Apollonian mentality of technocratic society, which
stresses rationality, discipline, delayed gratification, and living
for future rewards. A social order based predominantly on
reason and planning for optimum productivity leaves out too
many human values, especially those which are expressed in
symbolic gestures and feelings, in the language of art and love,
which cannot be reduced to prose or mathematics. He berates

the politics of the New Left for its unmitigated insistence on academic and ideological approaches to social issues: "Ideology is brain disease."[15] He opposes a social system based on ascetical denial that forces persons to adopt someone else's vision of the good life for the sake of material rewards.

The Dionysian impulse reminds people "to dig what you're doing,"[16] to have fun in life. The coming revolution must be born of joy, not sacrifice. Hoffman proposes a kind of theology of the clown by encouraging people to recapture the childlike qualities of spontaneity, directness, and wonder that have been stamped out by the regimentation and standards of Pig Nation. In this context, growing up often means giving up one's dreams; "Begin to live your vision,"[17] advocates Hoffman. The Dionysian attitude calls for a politics of ecstasy as a corrective to the politics of calculation and compromise. As might be expected from one so leery of rational definitions, Hoffman does not explain the "politics of ecstasy" other than to liken it to the art of living life authentically according to the real needs and inspirations of a person's integrated organism. Traditional politics frequently compels people to value themselves according to alien norms, the expectations and desires of others. The politics of ecstasy calls on a person to enjoy and express his own inner worth, his own self-valuation. Politics for Hoffman has mainly to do with the way someone lives his life rather than with political systems as these are generally understood.

Dionysian religiousness means living in a timeless now that transcends the common servitude in technocratic society to clocks and schedules. To be now is his chief concern as opposed to a future-directed existence that fills the present with anxiety and emptiness. This ability to fully relish the present also demands a freedom to be happy without having to be busy pursuing some specific task. It is a capacity to live "stoned." This does not necessarily involve psychedelic experience, although the latter is also related to Hoffman's religiousness. Without drugs the Dionysian man "has found the immense power inherent in changing one's own life, the power that comes from laughter, looseness, and the refusal to take seriously that which is rigid and nonhuman."[18] Because the future is now, for a Yippie, he can be optimistic and idealistic about the future. Those who cannot revel in the present moment of existence may be too fearful about the future to cope with it imaginatively or to expect that it will bring them anything better than their present trepidations.

The Dionysian perspective, in sum, comes to the fore in human affairs when the old order of things has become decadent and devoid of life-giving energies. In his modern frenzy, the Dionysian Hoffman is attempting to alert the nation about the demise of the old forms of social and personal coherence. And in his wild way he is pointing to new directions for making institutions and philosophies verdant again. He wants to exorcise himself and others of the paralyzing fears that arise when men are called to break with the familiar and traditional because they have become moribund. Yet it is not enough to theorize about this risky departure. The Dionysian requires the exuberance of the dance. Reason is inadequate to convince the human animal that he must move on to new life forms; he must sense this imperative with his whole body-person. He feels impelled to come into the streets and dance joyously on the grave of the old system; around the walls of the Pentagon he writes: "We will dance and sing and chant the mighty OM."[19]

It would be easy at this point to dismiss Hoffman's Dionysian élan as irresponsible madness or as a dubious exploit of frustrated liberals who lack the patience to work within the system. It could be pointed out that the system seems to defy the early obituaries pronounced by the Dionysians. The Pentagon still stands. Such judgments would indeed be true, but they also stunt imaginative flights of the human spirit straining to envision and create new possibilities. The Dionysian is not trying to construct a prudent analysis of the status quo. He desires to show the limits of a rationality that determines the future only on the merits of the past: "It's only when you get to the end of Reason can you begin to enter the Woodstock Nation."[20] Abbie Hoffman in his Dionysian-oriented life transcends his situation through the intensity, ecstasy, and precarious-ness that he experiences as he strains at the limit of his existence.

Psychedelic drugs are another device used to cultivate a new consciousness. LSD and marijuana form an integral part of Hoffman's life style, as is evident throughout his writings. The question of the relationship between drugs and the experience of religious transcendence has received considerable attention in modern times.[21] In the light of traditional spirituality, the main criticism of drugs as a mode of religious experience stems from the Pelagian, or self-induced, nature of the expanded conscious-ness. The religious element of grace, or gratuity, seems to be missing. Yet even in the context of the history of religious movements, drugs have been understood as factors that dispose the person to be open to novel awarenesses. In this sense, drugs might be related to fasting, penances, solitude, pilgrimages, and the Jesus Prayer as vehicles that dispose the religionist to enrich-ing perceptions of reality. In the conditioning of the counter-culture "monks," rock music is often combined with marijuana or other drugs. Against the rationality and detachment of "straight" technocratic society, the sound and visual effects of a rock concert envelop those present with passionate intensity and involvement. For Hoffman, mind-expanding drugs provide an opening to further possibilities of experience that were previously excluded by the dulling pressures of daily life in Pig Nation.

This does not imply a continual or excessive reliance on drugs nor a dependency on them as the only way to transcendent perceptions and insights. But drugs become one way to achieve a broadened consciousness that unlocks facets of reality that were hidden, especially in the one-dimensional patterns of tech-nocratic society. Some radical reformers, such as the Black Panthers, counsel strongly against the use of drugs because they turn the users into themselves and away from the struggles of the social and political revolution. Although this escapist, opiate effect is a real danger for the revolutionary, radicals such as Hoffman show that drug use can be combined with intense forms of political activism. His writings are filled with an active awareness of political, military, economic, and cultural issues in American life. The self-destructive use of drugs often results in personalities whose psychic make-up inclines them to unhealthy addictions, whether of alcohol, cigarettes, or dangerous drugs.

For Hoffman the drug experience seems to have value in terms of *metanoia* and self-liberation. The effect of drugs need not end when the drug itself wears off. A new degree of awareness and sensitivity can persist in a person's other activities. In the words of Reich: ". . . there may come a time when a drug user feels that drugs are no longer necessary to him, or at least that they have become of lesser importance; he has achieved the increased awareness he wanted and it is part of him now."[22] However optimistic this statement may be when generalized to all drug users, it does have relevance for Abbie Hoffman. Having tasted some of the fruits of new vistas through drugs, he wants to bring others to a consciousness in which they could question the destructive pursuits that pass for values in an aggressively competitive society.

A key means of self-transcendence for Hoffman is his wit and humor. Yet the laughable incongruities of his antics are welded to a very serious purpose—a radical reform of society and self. Hoffman embodies what can be called the religiousness of the clown. The prophetic jester pokes fun at himself and he ridicules the foibles of society. Such humor implies both a considerable humility and flexibility of personality and a commitment to disconcert a deadly serious society in its attempts to absolutize itself. Thus the jester must transcend his own locked-in self-importance and his self-aggrandizing schemes; he must also aid his fellows to avoid creating a vicious society of "power-freaks": "Maintain a sense of humor. People who take themselves too seriously are power-crazy. If they win, it will be haircuts for all. Beware of power-freaks."[23] Hoffman is willing to criticize the overly serious reformers on the left as well as on the right.

There is a profound religious dialectic at work in Hoffman's humor. It is the perennial struggle between the truth and

force of laughter over against the falsehood and apparent control
of the powerful. It is a kind of quixotic faith that laughter is
stronger and more sublime than technological mastery and political manipulation. Hoffman urges his readers to have a good
time and do weird things. He imagines Hitler with his pants
pulled down in Trafalgar Square: ". . . he could never have
risen to power . . . 'Mein Führer' with his pants down around
his ankles would have been too much. Think about it."[24] Nearly
all of Hoffman's zany political stunts have the quality of fun
about them. Fun involves the whole person: "I mean an experience so intense that you actualize your full potential. You
become life. Life is Fun."[25] Western culture, with its emphasis
on technological achievement, has deprived man of the full
potential he might enjoy in the fun of celebration and festivity.
Hoffman's humor, sometimes vulgar and strident, sometimes
subtle and sensitive, is the voice and gesture of the prophetic
jester who calls his audience to climb free of the shackles of
deadening seriousness and experience life as fun.

Direct political action, although in the Yippie style, becomes
still another method to attain personal self-transcendence, for
Hoffman. For all his spoofing of the political sphere, Hoffman
is very much involved in politics. Even a cursory tour through
his books reveals statements and actions relating to the major
national institutions. The New York Stock Exchange and the
capitalist system in general, the Pentagon and its wars, the presi-
dency, Congress, the urban crisis, the black revolution, the struggles of the Third World, poverty and the mass media—these
and many more structures and issues become the context of
direct Yippie political action.

But it is a different form of action from that which is com-
monly associated with getting things done in the political arena.
The latter consists in building respected roles, learning to con-
form and compromise, and waiting for the tactical moment to
wield power through accepted channels. Hoffman's political action is that of the outsider, the person who consciously stands
apart from the mentality and mores of the dominant culture of

the technocratic state. In his manner of speech and dress, in proposing illegal activities, he chooses to stand outside the system so as not to be co-opted by it. Every true Yippie is a runaway, an outlaw. He rejects the social roles of "straight" politics to foster his own independent consciousness of what must be done to change self and society. For those who make themselves outcasts by renouncing approved roles, the goals and rewards of the old ways with their social comfort and prestige must also be abandoned. Some critics of the counterculture dismiss this self-imposed alienation as a romanticist fling or as adolescent rebelliousness. Yet the hardship and loneliness attendant on rejection of approved roles is not sufficiently appreciated as a notable sacrifice in those who act as non-conformist political reformers. Again, however, it is important to distinguish between the dropping out of accepted social patterns that retreats from direct confrontation with political institutions and the purposeful dropping out of a Hoffman to better contend with political structures. He is essentially a political activist who has incorporated hippie modes and his own clowning talents into political action.

In the end, Hoffman, like Rubin, wants to do things that will bring about a deep change in the political and cultural order. The Yippie activist strives to create a political crisis. Says Rubin: "Our goal was to create crises which would grab everybody's attention and force people to change their lives overnight."[26] In the creation of crises, political action as a means of liberating self-transcendence comes to the fore. Just as the Yippie individual realized a measure of inner freedom by separating himself from the dominant culture, so, too, a political crisis situation becomes an occasion for social liberation. People are shaken out of familiar and mesmerizing ways; they are forced to think and act with more creative imagination. They are pressed to develop themselves when they are forced to work together, to become aware of needs to which they had been oblivious. In this manner political struggle for Hoffman becomes a significant talisman for self-transcendence; politics is in large measure the stuff of which his religious experience is made.

Radical politics, however, carries with it the dangers of any movement built largely on elements of idealistic projection. Ordinary political positions are based on the compromises and power plays of vested interests in concrete situations. Since radicalism belongs to the imagination of visionary possibilities in the world, it may never connect with this real political world. Or the radical may become disillusioned and frustrated at his attempts to effect change, and withdraw from the political stage. Yet there are indirect ways of relating to and altering the entrenched politics of the system. It is possible that aspects of the radical vision will influence liberal politicians who in turn may be able to effect specific changes. Whether the contemporary radicals have the patience and perseverance to communicate their revolutionary vision remains to be seen.

Abbie Hoffman's religious experience, as seen up to this point, centers on the Yippie version of self-transcendence—a total cultural and psychic liberation from the destructive aspects of the dominant society; it also implies freedom for self-realization in a new style of community. His motivating images of coherence and wonder are intrinsically tied to the means by which he fosters growth in liberating self-transcendence: the theatrical, the Dionysian, the psychedelic, the humorous, and the political. What can be said of his moral sense, the principles that guide his judgment of good and evil, and that motivate ethical decisions to act? Evil consists in all those elements of Pig Nation that impede inner liberation and the creation of a co-operative community. He sums up this vision of evil in the three R's against which the children of Woodstock Nation rebel: "they heard from their mothers over and over again about being *respectable, responsible* and above all, *reasonable.*"[27] Yet these high-sounding words were hypocritical subterfuges for conformity, prejudice, oppression, and authoritarianism, as the context of the same chapter brings out.

His moral stance rests on a consistent advocacy of an anarchist individualism over against authoritarian manipulation of people. The rulers of Pig Nation are generally oppressive to his sense of liberty. He reminds readers that Eichmann lived by the rules and that society needs cheerleaders more than authority figures. He urges followers to live by their own rules. For him, the ethical good is first and foremost an interior liberation of the self. It has to do with personal creativity, individuality, and enjoyment. The first commitment must be to self; true morality for Hoffman would foster the uniqueness and dignity of each individual, and it would respect his conscientious choices in the existential moment. Autocreativity and self-appreciation are the cornerstones of his anarchist morality.

Unless this central element of anarchist morality is grasped, there is little chance of empathizing with many of Hoffman's ethical positions. For him, much that is considered legal and responsible and respectable is linked to an authoritarian system that forces an individual to suppress the needs and potential of his own organism. The self is enslaved to school, family, church, state, and other institutions and persons. The fated self cannot shape his own destiny. Many would dismiss his irreverent antics and gross overstatements as the products of immaturity, egoism, and superficiality. A partial case can be made for such strictures. But to rest content with such estimates is to miss the value of an anarchist morality. Although it may involve illegality and defiance of social canons (e.g. the publishing furor over his latest book, *Steal This Book,* which advocates illegal acts), the anarchist construes his morality on a different primordial principle than that undergirding conventional morality.

The anarchist principle rests on the judgment that the given social system destroys individuality and creativity in the self (and indirectly in the community at large); therefore, the system must be opposed. This starting point for Hoffman's morality is exemplified at the beginning of his latest book. *Amerika* is pictured as a prison; the book is a survival manual and a guide for a jailbreak to a freer life for the self.[28] The anarchist is also interested in community, that is, a fellowship of free and sharing persons, but as a secondary extension of the liberated individual. What he fears most are authoritarian institutions or individuals that crush the inner creativity of the self and thus make community impossible. Hoffman's morality is as concerned about justice, honesty, freedom, and love as are the more conventional forms of ethics. But these virtues are reflected through the unusual prism of an anarchist jester's perspective. Since anarchy is often associated in the popular mind with chaos, license, and perversion of traditional values, the contribution of the authentic anarchist tends to be overlooked. He is the one who can remind a conformist, authoritarian, and alienated society that its highest moral aspirations will be stifled unless much more attention is given to the uninhibited unfolding of the unique self.

Hoffman's morality is action oriented: ". . . one realizes that action is the only reality; not only reality but morality as well."[29] This action ethics is opposed to moral systems based on ideological principles and conventional codes, as these mandates are imposed from outside the self. Hoffman's morality is eminently situational in the sense that the right or good action will result if a person follows his impulses and acts in response to the concrete needs of the moment. Rubin puts it starkly: "Act first. Analyze later. Impulse—not theory—makes the great leaps forward."[30] Hoffman speaks of: ". . . letting go. Losing control. Just doing what pops into my mind. I trust my impulses. I find the less I try to think through a situation, the better it comes off."[31] Hoffman, who attempts to live a theatrical and Dionysian existence, emphasizes the symbolic richness of action involving the whole person over against abstract speculation.

A dual dimension can be consistently found in this action-oriented ethic: the action and the self, or, better, the acting self, forms the chief criterion for right and wrong conduct. The first stress is on doing; the second aspect focuses on the self: *do your own* thing. Technological society shudders at the thought of such an ethic because it threatens a civilization established on control of instinct and careful regimentation of impulse. Hoffman's ethic is the nemesis of a computerized culture. In one sense, his action morality would undo many of the benefits that society has achieved through reflective planning, social control, and accountability. This is especially true of highly complex modern societies. But it is precisely a civilization dedicated to computerized security that needs to hear Hoffman's message of a basic trust in the feelings and impulses of one's own organism. Such a morality manifests a fundamental faith in the worth of man's instincts at a time when people are increasingly subjected to machines in technocratic culture.

The Yippie ethic's very optimism about the transcendent possibilities of the liberated self reveals its lack of profound appreciation for the tragic dimensions of man's existential situation. This is not to say that Hoffman is oblivious of real evils in the world; on the contrary, his writings are constantly holding up a mirror to the hypocrisy and injustice of Pig Nation. But there is little empathy in his works for the existential dilemmas of temporality, contingency, and mortality. This might be attributable to the healthy vigor of youth coupled with an anarchist's optimism about the liberated self. Hoffman, like other revolutionaries, attempts to cope with the existential limit of death. He shows bravery in his willingness to face death in the pursuit of a changed society. Living in constant fear of death is to him a far worse fate than dying itself. Yet his brash and sometimes swaggering style gives little indication of compassion for human suffering and weakness. This is the most outstanding flaw in his whole morality. More than anything else, this dearth of compassion for suffering and failure in self and society gives pause about the viability of the new society based on the values of Woodstock Nation.

Hoffman's morality, stemming from the flower and fun aspects of the Yippie credo, is largely nonviolent. He maintains that Pig Nation is ever prone to military and police violence. In general his countertactics to the threat of violence are ridicule and humor acted out with Yippie histrionics. He wants to carry flowers into St. Patrick's Cathedral in protest against a hawkish cardinal. In opposition to police use of Mace, he urges "Lace" as a love potion to facilitate the exorcism and levitation of the Pentagon. Perhaps the most indicative statement about Hoffman's view of violence is the following: "Although I admire the revolutionary art of the Black Panthers, I feel that guns alone will never change this system. You don't use a gun on an IBM computer. You pull the plug out."[32] Although he does not elaborate a principled stand for nonviolence, his comic spirit seems less oriented to violent response.

Moreover, an unexpected practicality reveals itself in Hoffman's attitude toward violence. He really doesn't believe that guns and ideology alone will work to bring about the changes he desires. In contrast to Rubin on this point, Hoffman at the 1968 Democratic Convention wanted to show both the clenched fist and the smile, the gun and the flower. Yet Hoffman is willing to resort to violence if it is necessary to preserve the existence of the counterculture movement. He maintains that only as much force as is necessary should be used. Yet he finds that the movement has had to become more militant in order to survive: "To love we must survive, to survive we must fight."[33] Of necessity the flower children have grown thorns. The theme of struggling for survival even by violent means is reiterated in *Steal This Book*. Hoffman in the 1970s claims that he would never again appear with a toy gun, as he did on the cover of *Revolution for the Hell of It*. At times he seems to be moving toward a position of direct struggle and confrontation with a regime that he deeply mistrusts. More recently, however, Hoffman has been heard to urge support of progressive candidates for election. Perhaps this apparent contradiction is another example of Yippie creative confusion. But the ultimate criterion determining the use of violence in the Yippie ethic is consistent with its anarchist stance. To protect the uniqueness and dignity of the individual, the conscientious demands of the existential moment should be followed.

Yet this situational ethic, when joined to plans for theft and even violence, as in his latest book, can lead to furthering the very destructive violence that Hoffman decries in Pig Nation.

The book is aimed at helping movement people survive in an unjust society whose wage and tax system is deeply rooted in domestic and foreign exploitation. Yet to survive by the same means as the dehumanizing, dominant society is also to dehumanize the resisters and make their goals for a new social order less likely. The challenge is not simply to survive, but to do so in such a way that begins to portray in the very style of resistance a co-operative, honest, nonviolent fellowship. This higher human purpose is an overriding theme within the whole context of Hoffman's Yippie pursuits. But *Steal This Book* tends to undermine the community of Woodstock Nation and set it on the alienating road of violence, cunning, consumerism, and power-seeking characteristic of Pig Nation.

Hoffman's self-transcendent experiences through his Yippie symbols of coherence, wonder, and morality are an incessant pursuit of freedom. The words "freedom" and "liberation" have been the central focus at every step in the career of Abbie Hoffman. "Free is the essence of yippie!"[34] On one level, "free" means access to goods and services without payment. As a witness against the materialistic values and hoarding spirit of Pig Nation, Hoffman talks about free stores, free cities, free society. But this dimension of freedom is only the external sign of a spiritual and interior freedom that forms the core of Yippie anarchism. This freedom is a liberation of heart and mind from the theories and practices of technocratic society that smother individual growth, enjoyment, and creativity. In brief, the positive goal of freedom is "do your thing." In the same chapter, Hoffman illustrates the contrast between unfreedom and freedom by referring to Eichmann and Abraham. Eichmann became a slave of the rules, conforming himself to an external deity, a machine, a system. Abraham trusted his own impulses, thus discovering God's freedom within himself. For Hoffman, by liberating the inner self and by acting with trust of inner impulses, man becomes free, becomes divine. At its most profound level, the religious experience in Hoffman's life pertains to the experience of freedom, which opens him to transcendent possibilities for life enhancement and unifies him more coherently with the universe.

Although the freedom of the individual self is the chief consideration of Hoffman's religiousness, he does not lose sight of community. The self can realize its freedom only in community, not as an isolated being. Hoffman states: ". . . the revolution is about coming together in a struggle for change . . . it is about the building of a new community based on people and cooperation."[85] The liberated individual is committed to the pursuit of greater liberation both for himself and for others. There is almost a fervor about recruiting new members for the community: "the first line of defense is to turn on the enemy . . . under the uniform of a cop exists a naked human being."[86] In marches, the call goes out to bystanders to join the movement.

The basis for Hoffman's motivating vision of a new community rests on the rejection of a competitive, profit-oriented society for one of co-operation and participation. Capitalism, as he sees it, leads to the destruction of true community, because it engenders the alienation of persons from themselves and from others. The hoarding of property and the maximizing of profit become the main preoccupations of life. People are manipulated for the gain, power, and prestige of the wealthy class, and work becomes a depressing drudgery for the sake of money. This analysis of the anti-communitarian aspects of capitalist society resembles the standard socialist or Marxist critique. But Hoffman believes that most brands of Marxism, which substitute state for corporate bureaucratic control, are as harmful for the United States as is capitalism. Although he sees intimations of the new community in the Cuban revolution, the National Liberation Front, and the radical youth movements, the truly new style of community is yet to be built.

Although the Yippies assert that the new community exists now where free individuals act in concert, this concept is more of an empowering futurist symbol than a present reality. Hoffman's reflection on a particularly good meeting of movement people elicited perhaps the best short description of what the new community could be: "Ours is a circle: respect, love, trust."[87] Such a community would be a place of participational democracy aimed at consensus and co-operation. This new community, according to Hoffman, will not be structured along the traditional dividing lines of age, nation, class, and race. The universality of the global village will know only attitudinal differences: "When you see another hippie in the street . . . you smile and say hello—a kind of comradeship that I've seen black people show when they are alone in the white world."[88] This utopian vision acts as a lure toward new realizations of self-transcendence, for Hoffman. As an ideal conception, it plays an important part in his religious experience.

But, in the context of Hoffman's anarchist theories and specific practices, important obstacles arise to the fashioning of his hoped-for community. These problems cluster around the question of freedom among freedoms in a community. First, his lack of compassion for persons different from himself bespeaks a mentality that might want to suppress diversity and dissent in a community where the Hoffmans and Rubins dominate. Hoffman's stress on self-fulfillment, on doing your own thing, can lead to a self-centeredness deleterious to building community. The freedom of the self to become according to its full potential cannot be divorced from the limitations inexorably imposed on the self by the rights of others to exercise their freedoms. Doing one's thing is a cardinal virtue in Hoffman's lexicon; this self-expression is joined to a strong renunciation of self-sacrifice. His position contains much merit as an antidote to guilt-ridden asceticism, but it harbors problems for developing community. It is doubtful that any lasting community can be maintained without a love that demands at times self-sacrifice. There is an important distinction between sacrificing oneself in the sense of "giving up" one's selfhood and *giving of* oneself in the sense of sharing and suffering with and for others. The latter notion is not totally absent from Hoffman's outlook, but it tends to be suppressed in his strong emphasis on individualism. It is somewhat ironical that such an uncompromising opponent of capitalist individualism reaffirms this very quality in an anarchist understanding.

These difficulties concerning the building of community are almost inevitable, given Hoffman's primary focus on the liberated self. The real essence of the community is still the individual. Communal responsibility and commitment are secondary to the anarchist's vision of self-realization: ". . . [community is] just a lot of guys whose heads are in the same place but with different styles."[89] Despite its inherent problems, however, the dream of a liberated self in a free community is the central motivating symbol that opens Abbie Hoffman to transcendent possibilities. It is clearly an unrealized and open-ended symbol that requires an optimistic outlook on the potential of humans to live in brotherhood and peace. Yet it is precisely this imaginative invention of a more blessed world that underlies the religiousness of Hoffman's life direction. When a man creates his own fictions and lives by them, he not only reflects his own needs and hopes, but he also manifests his unrelenting quest for participation in the mystery of unconditioned knowledge and love.

The religious experience in Hoffman's life style of self-liberation points to a kind of divine presence in man. For him the divinization of man is blocked by technocratic society, which tends to alienate man by reducing him to a machine: "Inside he knows because He is God, which is to say, a Man and not a machine."[40] There is an important link between Hoffman's myth of freedom revolution and his reference to Camus that we have but one way of creating God, which is to become Him. The main phases of Hoffman's Yippie existence constitute a quest for transcendence, a will to participate in or "become" divinity through worldly self-integration. This transcendence is not to be defined in a narrowly orthodox religious sense but in a broader, anthropological perspective. Yippie drama, humor, drugs, and other Dionysian strivings are attempts to discover or create a reintegrated person of mind and body, passion and purpose, reason and unconscious, self and community. Such divinizing of man need not be understood as a crass form of pantheism, which fails to distinguish between the godly and un-godly aspects of reality. Rather, Hoffman's quest for wholeness through Yippie symbols is a striking contemporary manifestation of an ageless longing to participate in a richer realm of existence, which man has perennially associated with divinity. Hoffman's revolution is really not for the hell of it.

Footnotes

1. Abbie Hoffman, *Woodstock Nation* (New York: Vintage Books, 1969), p. 7.
2. *Woodstock*, p. 1.
3. Charles A. Reich, *The Greening of America* (New York: Random House, 1970), p. 254.
4. Abbie Hoffman (Free), *Revolution for the Hell of It* (New York: Dial Press, 1968), p. 35.
5. *Woodstock*, p. 75.
6. Jerry Rubin, *Do It!* (New York: Ballantine Books, 1970), pp. 86, 132.
7. *Greening*, p. 225.
8. *Woodstock*, p. 8.
9. Ibid.
10. *Do It!*, p. 115.
11. *Revolution*, p. 101.
12. *Revolution*, p. 26.
13. *Revolution*, p. 27.
14. *Revolution*, p. 101.
15. *Revolution*, p. 56.
16. *Revolution*, p. 10.
17. *Revolution*, p. 61.
18. *Greening*, p. 344.
19. *Revolution*, p. 39.
20. *Woodstock*, p. 133.
21. Aldous Huxley, in *The Doors to Perception,* at times clothes his phrases about the psychedelic experience in terms of religious mysticism. In *The Psychedelic Review* a number of contemporary writers have explored the phenomenon of expanded consciousness through drugs as a transcendent experience.
22. *Greening*, p. 260.
23. *Revolution*, p. 153.
24. *Revolution*, p. 31.
25. *Revolution*, p. 62.
26. *Do It!*, p. 37.
27. *Woodstock*, p. 18.

28. Abbie Hoffman, *Steal This Book* (New York: Grove Press, 1971), pp. iii ff.
29. *Revolution,* p. 9.
30. *Do It!,* p. 116.
31. *Revolution,* p. 63.
32. *Revolution,* p. 183.
33. *Woodstock,* p. 112.
34. *Revolution,* p. 147.
35. *Woodstock,* p. 71.
36. *Revolution,* p. 154.
37. *Revolution,* p. 37.
38. *Revolution,* p. 34.
39. *Revolution,* p. 50.
40. *Revolution,* p. 11.

Bibliography

Hoffman, Abbie. *Revolution for the Hell of It.* New York: Dial Press, 1968.
——. *Woodstock Nation.* New York: Vintage Books, 1969.
——. *Steal This Book.* New York: Grove Press, 1971.
Rubin, Jerry. *Do It!* New York: Simon & Schuster, 1970.
Reich, Charles. *The Greening of America.* New York: Random House, 1970.
Roszak, Theodore. *The Making of a Counter Culture.* New York: Double-day & Co., 1969.

VII - Frantz Fanon

Few revolutionary figures have been as influential as Frantz Fanon. In the decade since his death, he has become a leading spokesman for the liberation struggles of Third World countries, and he has strongly inspired radical movements in the Western world. Through his experiences in Martinique and Algeria, he was able to articulate both the alienation and the aspirations of oppressed people, giving them a new awareness of their situation and revolutionary insights for changing their world. Fanon presents a unique combination of qualities as an analyst of and a participant in the successful revolution of the Algerians against the French. As a black intellectual, he understood the depths of racism pervading the colonial environment; as a doctor and psychiatrist, he explored the psychic and emotional ramifications of racism in both the native and the settler. He was a writer and journalist who animated the Algerian resistance and awakened a consciousness of the possibilities of African unity. He was a military doctor-diplomat who knew firsthand the dangers of treating his fellow rebels and the risks of being an ambassador for a rebel cause. Fanon's experience of self-transcendence is remarkably lucid both on the level of psychological scrutiny of the changing self and also on the plane of societal upheavals and transformations. His life and work constitute an especially rich reservoir for studying the religious experience as personal self-transcendence toward freedom in community.

Fanon was born in 1925 in Fort-de-France, a town on the French Caribbean island of Martinique. As a freethinker and Freemason in a dominantly Catholic milieu, Fanon's father provided a home atmosphere in which the young Fanon developed a strong sense of independence and a thirst for liberty. In school he was particularly interested in philosophical subjects; his intellectualist bent led him from the empirical aspects of medicine to concentration on the psychological. After serving with the Free French forces during World War II, he entered medical school in Lyons and moved on to become a highly regarded psychiatrist. In Martinique he had come under the influence of the poet of negritude, Aimé Césaire, whose writings extol the beauty and value of blackness in the midst of a colonial culture that denigrated the Negro. Césaire helped Fanon to question and explore the desires of West Indian blacks to reject their own heritage and strive to become French in language, mannerisms, and thought. In the light of this formative influence, he was especially sensitive to the racist attitudes that he confronted in medical school and as a result of his marriage to a white woman. His first book, *Black Skin, White Masks,* reflects the experience of the young doctor outraged by the destructive psychic effects of self-hatred induced by colonial racism. Fanon's pursuit of liberation from the spurious quest for whiteness formed an important dimension of his religious self-transcendence.

From the time that Fanon accepted an appointment as a psychiatrist at Blinda, in Algeria, his understanding of revolutionary transcendence expanded from introspection to militant action, from psychiatry to politics. His first book, *Black Skin, White Masks,* revealed impressively the process of inner disalienation of the self, but his classic volume, *The Wretched of the Earth,* published shortly before his untimely death from leukemia in 1961, demonstrated Fanon as socialist revolutionary. It is not that he rejects psychological explanations for racism and colonial exploitation. Rather, he incorporates and enlarges his psychological insights into a broader vision for social revolution; for he comes to realize that only through such a total transformation of self and society can full human liberation be achieved. As the war with France intensified, Fanon's activities with the revolutionaries made his position in the hospital more precarious. In a trenchant and emotional letter of resignation, he attacked French racism toward North Africans. After his expulsion from Algeria, in 1957, Fanon went to Tunis, where he wrote articles for FLN publications. His unsigned pieces form a passionate and critical indictment of colonialism and the sufferings it was imposing on millions of Algerians. In his services as an ambassador for the provisional Algerian government, he narrowly escaped ambush and assassination. It was during these voyages that his dreams of a united Africa took shape; he urged the solidarity of all Africans against the yoke of colonialism. But by 1960 his final illness was sapping his energies, and he raced bravely against time to finish *The Wretched of the Earth,* by which his revolutionary spirit has been communicated throughout the world.

The general scheme of Frantz Fanon's pattern of self-transcendence involves a threefold movement. The Manichaean structure of colonial society must be overthrown by a period of reverse Manichaeism, the stage of violent revolution, to culminate in a resolution of polemic dualisms during the third moment of socialist reconciliation. Fanon describes the inner self-transformations and the societal transcendence as these evolve in each period. The old Manichaeism denies the possibilities for authentic self-transcendence on a personal or communal level. For the sake of selfish gain through controlled exploitation, the settler sees himself and his values as superior; the native and his ways are inferior and evil. As a psychiatrist, Fanon is able to articulate the forms of alienation that characterize this first period. He endeavors to free himself and his patients, black and white, from the slavery of the old Manichaeism.

But most of Fanon's thought and activity as an active participant in the Algerian revolt falls into the second phase, that of the violent overthrow of the oppressive culture of the settlers. In the process he formulates a neo-Manichaeism of the native toward the colonizers. During this time, a populist mystique, similar to that of Guevara, motivates bloody resistance against the colonial powers. In the course of describing the second, or actively revolutionary, period, Fanon also speaks about the third stage—of a new humanity, new history, and new man. These symbols become the objective images that inspire his religious experience. Another way of stating the dialectic of self-transcendence for Fanon is that a revolutionary present struggles for liberation from an oppressive past (together with the freeing of suppressed values of the native past) for the sake of a future social order of transcendent possibilities. Fanon's subjective motivating symbols of coherence, wonder, and morality are nuanced differently in each of the three moments of the general dialectical pattern of self-transcendence through the overcoming of Manichaeism.

Under the conditions of the old Manichaeism, constructive self-transcendence toward growth in freedom is greatly impeded. For a neurotic ambiguity is imposed on the native by the ruling colonial classes. By the time the Antillean or the Algerian comes to recognize himself as an adult Negro, he has been educated by the foreign culture to equate being black with the "wicked, sloppy, instinctual and malicious."[1] During the years of domination, the French objectified the Arab and the Negro; all the qualities that are native to them have been cast in a negative and repulsive light. The black as black is emptied of his substance, and the model of humanity and civilization becomes the Frenchman. The native represents not only the absence of values, but also their negation: "He is . . . the enemy of values, and in this sense he is absolute evil. He is the corrosive element, destroying all that comes near him; he is the deforming element, disfiguring all that has to do with beauty or morality; he is the depository of maleficent powers. . . ."[2] The settler dehumanizes the native and conceives of him in animal terms.

Under pretense of preserving native values, the colonialists objectify the native into categories of inferior value in comparison with French culture. The native is thus robbed of his substance, and he is reduced to a confused and self-hating creature who can be manipulated for the profit of the settlers. While it is of antiquarian interest to catalogue native lore and artifacts, it is essential that the colonial system make the native admit the supremacy of the white man's values. The settler writes his own history, not that of the natives; the point must be incessantly made in overt and subtle ways that to save the race it must be whitened. It is not only important that the educated native speak French, but that he eliminate as fully as possible all traces of foreign accent, lest he be relegated to an inferior standing. Fanon himself felt even more intensely the crushing weight of racism when he went to Europe. There he was classified as a Negro, even though his earlier education had conditioned him to consider himself an Antillean, in contrast to the blacks of Africa. He realized through his own inner sufferings that the black man is locked in an infernal circle of self-defeating insignificance and inadequacy: "When people like me they tell me it is in spite of my color. When they dislike me, they point out that it is not because of my color. Either way, I am locked into the infernal circle."[3]

The institutions of colonial society foster the racism that acts as a legitimating and controlling factor for continued exploitation. The police and the army are viewed by Fanon as custodians of an oppressive status quo; they act as go-betweens for the settler in his relations with the natives. Thus the symbols of physical power tend to reinforce the psychic and cultural images of colonial dominance in the mind and subconscious of the natives. Schools and churches also indoctrinate and pacify the native. At the cost of grave and neurotic self-alienation, the educational and cultural institutions teach the Algerian to substitute white values for black ones in order that he may rise into the native bourgeoisie. For the sake of profit and prestige during the period of colonial Manichaeism, such blacks become traitors to their own people and ape the white culture. The legal system is also constructed to maintain the hegemony of the ruling foreign classes; gradually the repressive laws of the settler provoke the natives to deeper resentment and prepare them for the emancipating revolution.

It is important to reflect on these social instruments of control and manipulation, because the dialectic of revolutionary self-transcendence is put in motion against the dehumanizing pressures of the regnant colonial empire. On this topic a significant analogy exists with traditional religious literature; for example, Hebrew communal self-transcendence was partially the result of reaction to foreign domination. St. Paul's religious transformation takes place in opposition to the spiritual powers that control the universe. Ironically, the Christian church, which claims to be a vehicle for the Pauline message of liberation, becomes for Fanon still another social instrument of repression. He puts it succinctly: "The Church in the colonies is the white people's Church, the foreigner's Church. She does not call the native to God's ways but to the ways of the white man, of the master, of the oppressor."[4] A religious experience toward freedom in community cannot be cultivated by the native population in churches that work to fit him into a system of self-destruction.

Such social institutions thrust the native more deeply into the zone of neurotic self-hatred. For Fanon this state of chaos and ambiguity in the self can be likened to a condition of sin, of irreligion. The native is caught in chains forged by conflicting forces. He is envious of the settler and needs his approbation. Yet he secretly hates the colonist, while at the same time the native rejects his own inner value. This plight of the black man in white society is sharply portrayed in Fanon's own life. His own identity crisis was only gradually resolved through active involvement in the Algerian struggle. The religiously redeeming ability to accept himself awaits the revolution, which allows the native to sense, perhaps for the first time, his own inner worth.

During the period of the old Manichaeism, the native tries to seek avenues of self-transcendence that turn out to be dead ends. He participates in frenzied rites of ancient religions in an attempt to release the conflicting energies within. He dreams of performing great physical exploits such as jumping across a river or leaping down from a mountain. As a psychiatrist, Fanon perceives clearly the close relationship between mental frustration and bodily reactions. The native also lashes out at his black brothers in violent ways, as he strives to displace the terrible angers that he cannot hope to vent on the French settlers. These very actions only serve to classify him as vicious in the mind of the ruling classes. The native longs to become white by making love to a white woman. Fanon describes this experience as a high point of the denial of blackness in the pursuit of white culture and beauty: "When my restless hands caress those white breasts, they grasp white civilization and dignity and make them mine."[5] This desire of the alienated black is judged in a different manner by the French settler. The latter projects onto the native an excess of sexual desire, identifying him with "lower" and animalistic elements. The powers of the body that disconcert the settler, who sees himself as part of an intellectual culture, are associated with the Algerian, who incorporates the principle of evil. Thus, in the colonial stituation, the very path of liberation from blackness and alienation becomes the route of increased debasement for the native.

In his earlier years as a psychiatrist, Fanon devoted himself to the redemption of blacks from the circle of self-alienation by applying the psychological methods of his profession. His goals were to free the black from the inferiority complexes that a rapacious system had inflicted on his brothers. Even before his encounters with racism in medical school, he recalled vividly the demeaning caste system based on race in his native Martinique. He was also deeply affected during the Second World War by the sight of Arab children eating out of the garbage cans of the French forces in North Africa. As a young psychiatrist, Fanon believed that the way of individual therapy, with its enlightenment and motivation to change, would suffice to "disalienate" the black. He speaks about setting the Negro on the road to disalienation as the purpose of his work as a native doctor. At this time the heart of his religious experience was rooted in the commitment to free himself and others from the neurotic situation of black alienation in a white culture.

Fanon described this life direction as a quest to "rise above this absurd drama that others have staged around me."[6] This going beyond the plight of self-hating alienation is the key to his personal self-transcendence as it manifested itself under the aegis of the old Manichaeism. It was necessary, in the poetic language of Césaire, to cut beneath the white paint on the bark and to find again the strength of blackness in the dark roots of the tree. Already the notes of violence that would later characterize Fanon's revolutionary thought are discernible in his citations from Césaire. Once the native had revealed to himself the white man's alienating veneer over the black self, he would gain his complete release from the sin of racism by killing the settler. Fanon quotes from Césaire a passage that is fraught with religious meaning in the wider humanistic context of this study. The faithful slave enters his master's quarters and the following scene ensues:

> "It is you," he said to me, quite calmly. . . . It was I. It was indeed I, I told him, the good slave . . . and suddenly his eyes were two frightened cockroaches on a rainy day . . . I struck, the blood flowed: That is the only *baptism* that I remember today.[7]

The slave affirms strongly that it was indeed himself; he had found the identity that the psychiatrist strove to help him discover. But his baptism, the rite of emancipation from his sinful state, was not complete by mere verbal proclamation of his new identity. The native, whom Fanon saw as a person of integrated mind and body, would not be satisfied with thought and word alone, severed from action. Fanon explicitly rejected such a dichotomy as a harmful result of European rationalism. The rite of release from alienation had to be finished by the physical action of killing the source of his enslavement. That it was the only baptism the native remembered indicates its central importance as a religious act of self-transcendence. Real liberation for transcendent life possibilities did not stem from the old rites and mysteries of native religion. Rather, it issued from contending directly with the all-encompassing, worldly phenomena of racism and exploitation.

The religious experience of self-transcendence for Fanon in his pre-Algerian years focused on the liberation of the individual from the oppression of a false consciousness formed in a racist environment. The emphasis is principally on the emancipation of the individual self through psychological therapy. Society intervenes as an essential backdrop for individual enslavement and liberation. But the full realization that psychic freedom for individuals could not be separated from radical social transformation awaited Fanon's political experiences in Algeria. His writings in North Africa manifest a new awareness that the psychological illnesses of the black man's feelings of inferiority and of non-existence could not be healed without a thoroughgoing social and political revolution. Racist alienation could not be cured unless its roots in political domination and economic exploitation were attacked. In the mid-1950s a transition occurred in Fanon's thought as the Algerian rebels struck out against the colonizers. The psychiatrist, concerned primarily with the disalienation of the individual, became the social revolutionary conspiring with the FLN to expel the French. Fanon came to understand that individual therapy was inadequate or even meaningless if the end result was only to aid the slave to cope with or fit into an essentially alienating system. As a *chef de service* in the mental hospital at Blinda in Algeria, he became politically radicalized. The torture and murder of Algerians by the French impelled him into closer collaboration with the rebel cause. It was no longer enough for him to labor at reforming mental health programs; the time for risky political action had arrived.

A related facet of Fanon's transition from individual therapy to social reconstruction was his rejection of the negritude movement as a solution for racial alienation. The return to an appreciation of negritude in art and culture marked an important development among blacks in the quest for authentic self-identity. Fanon remarks that prior to the arrival of Aimé Césaire in Martinique, the educated West Indians imitated the literature, music, and culture of white Europe. The Antillean carefully distinguished himself from the African Negro, who was considered a lower-class person. It was Césaire who taught the post World War II generation to cultivate their black heritage and to be proud of their blackness. Fanon admired the contribution of the negritude movement under the inspiration of Césaire: ". . . people joined him in chanting the once-hated song to the effect that it is fine and good to be a Negro!"[8]

Fanon, however, came to judge the black man's quest for the values of his ancestors as a helpful but intermediary stage in the struggle for liberation. During the phase of colonization, the native intellectual first tries to assimilate himself to the culture of the occupying nation. A second time is marked by the native's search for his own roots in folklore and art. The negative dimension of this worthwhile pursuit for Fanon rests on a certain passive satisfaction with past history without confronting the present issues of the freedom struggle. The native intellectual is thus able to be distracted from the task of social transformation by directing his talents to the cultivation of the past glories of negritude. Writing as a revolutionary journalist in Tunis in 1960, Fanon notes that even Césaire, whom he so respected in former years, had given his approval to De Gaulle's referendum, which would have kept the Caribbean islands as French domains. Fanon rejoices that the Antilleans reacted against such an

acquiescent and anti-revolutionary move. Here Fanon underscores the limitations of negritude: it fails to assume its active
political responsibilities in the present battle against oppression
and thus allows a basically alienating situation to continue. It
is only when the artist and the intellectual develop a politically
revolutionary consciousness that they can become awakeners of
the people through a new form of cultural expression. They
then become "the mouthpiece of a new reality in action."[9]

Frantz Fanon's transcendence of individualism in therapy
and negritude in cultural activities exemplifies a fundamental
position on human nature that undergirds each stage of his life.
His view of man is dynamic according to an existentialist and
dialectical perspective. He firmly rejects theories of man by
which he is destined to live within the confines of given norms
whether these be the prescriptions of a natural law or the codes
of the state. Moreover, he renounces an ideology of societal
development that proceeds according to a dialectical method that
"assumes the appearance of an absolutely inevitable mecha-
nism."[10] In place of deterministic views of man and society,
Fanon proposes an existentialist stance of free, self-creative
human activity in history. He sees himself as a searcher and
creator:

> There are in every part of the world men who search. I
> am not a prisoner of history. I should not seek there for
> the meaning of my destiny. I should constantly remind
> myself that the real *leap* consists in introducing invention
> into existence. In the world through which I travel, I am
> endlessly creating myself.[11]

Throughout his writings, he displays a signal sense of self-
transcendence through self-initiated activity. This pattern is evident in the stage of psychological liberation from racism as well
as in the revolutionary phase of decolonization. For him, history is not foreclosed; and his motivating symbols for action
on the levels of meaning, affection, and ethics are eminently

open-ended. He is caught up in a life process, a *metanoia,* of "going beyond": "I am part of Being to the degree that I go beyond it."[12]

Fanon's vision of the human person as a self-transcendent being is not only understood in terms of existentialist self-creativity but also as a dialectical process. To be fully human, each person must gain a consciousness of his own dignity and inner worth. This intrinsic sense of value is gained, according to Fanon, in a dialectic of recognition between persons that comes only after confrontation of people who mutually appreciate each other as human beings. Such recognition, he affirmed, following upon a real dialectic encounter, has never happened to the Negro. The master class has simply given blacks various concessions. These were aimed not at fostering mutual recognition, but at increasing the work output of Negroes. Thus the black has not really participated in the contest for his recognition.

By modifying the Hegelian understanding of the master-slave relation to suit his own purposes, Fanon lays the dialectical underpinnings for the need to rebel against the person and society of the white master. This philosophical and psychological explanation will later be corroborated by political theories of violent opposition. But it is important to notice that Fanon's dialectic understanding of man consists of more than negative reactions. Man is also actional, "preserving in all his relations his respect for the basic values that constitute a human world."[13] If man wishes to go beyond resentment toward his opponents, he must foster the "yes" as well as the "no" of the dialectic. Indeed, man is a *no: "No* to the scorn of man. *No* to degeneration of man . . . *No* to the butchery of what is most human in man: freedom." Yet man is also a *yes* to life, love, and generosity.[14] The whole thrust of this dialectic is to produce an expanding self-consciousness, a recognition of the self as a primal value.

Fanon came to realize, however, that such self-transcendence to freer modes of being was impossible under the conditions of colonial domination, with its racist ways. Even in his earlier works, he intimates the need for revolutionary struggle to achieve the positive outcomes of the dialectic of self-development. The black would have to reject the present arrangement as definite in order to bring about his disalienation. In a colonist culture, appeals to human dignity or to reason would not alter the Negro's lot. The settlers were too convinced of the superiority of their own persons and civilization to radically change their views of blacks. Moreover, the colonial system was based on the exploitation of the natives for economic gain to the settlers. The latter were not about to give up their power and wealth. As early as 1952, in his first book, Fanon asserted that there was but one solution left to the Negro: to fight. Yet it was not until his Algerian experience, where the viciousness and brutality of colonial domination of native peoples was a daily reality, that Fanon fully embraced the violent response of his neo-Manichaean period. The French use of torture against the native population to exact confessions or information especially revolted him; this revulsion was only compounded when no convictions were handed down to the torturers. As the Algerian war intensified, Fanon became convinced that in an environment of systematized dehumanization, true liberation meant total change of the social order.

In the second period of Fanon's career, he upholds the doctrine of reverse or neo-Manichaeism toward the colonial presence. The Manichaeism of the settler produced the response of Manichaeism in the native. It was not enough for the native to come to a psychological understanding of his repressed angers and violent fantasies. For release from his psychic and social alienation demanded that he vent these deep frustrations directly against the flesh of the settler. Fanon advocated the drastic solution of unrelenting violence to drive the oppressor from the land. New native life, he held, can only spring out of the rotting corpse of the settler. A kind of death/resurrection symbolism is at work in Fanon's neo-Manichaeism. The source of evil, the settler's value system and life style, must be killed to permit the long-oppressed native to realize his true identity and fashion a society of transcendent possibilities.

Fanon's symbolism here departs significantly from that of classic Christianity in which a Saviour figure suffers death and opens the way to resurrection for others. The way of Jesus is that of nonviolence, of overcoming the principle of evil by suffering under it with forgiveness and love. Fanon's use of this symbolism is more participational and less vicarious. His understanding of death/resurrection imagery coincides well with his unitary, or integrated, way of explaining the black man's nature. In contrast to the white man's separation of mind and body, thought and action, Fanon maintained that the Negro lived as a unity of the physical and the mental; he was the coupling of earth and consciousness. For him, revolutionary action entailed a participation of the whole person. It was not sufficient to allow a vicar or mediator to take the place of others. Redemption from the bondage of racism and colonialism called for direct action of the total human being, who would be freed.

The radical upheaval essential to Fanon's understanding of revolution implies a complete calling into question of the colonial situation. The whole foreign structure must be overthrown from the bottom up; the natives were to vomit up the values of the settlers. In Fanon's outlook, there can be no individual or social transcendence without the creation of a crisis situation. To go beyond a past condition of alienation, a vigorous discontinuity with colonialism must be established. This thoroughgoing revolution takes place on two levels, that of structures and that of values. He believed that the military struggle against the French would bring about a new order of political, economic, and social institutions. But the revolution remained unfinished unless a revaluation of values went along concomitantly with guerrilla warfare. All religious conversion, or *metanoia*, requires a breaking with past values, a discontinuity with structures and attitudes that have hardened into absolutes. The colonial culture became just such an absolute standard by which all life was judged. The deified system of the colonists and their black lackeys had to be shattered; France had become the religion and the God of these dominant classes. Thus the forming of a revolutionary crisis situation and its discontinuity with past values should be understood as a key fulcrum for Fanon's religious experience of self-transcendence.

The vehicle of shaping the revolutionary crisis and of fashioning new values for Fanon is mainly the peasantry. His populist mystique is similar to that of Che Guevara, in that the rural peasants form the chief body of revolutionary action. It is the peasantry that has nothing to lose and everything to gain in the all-out struggle against colonialism. The city proletarians have been divided and weakened by their close, servant relationship to the dominant white economic forces. This departure from classic Marxist theory about the industrial proletariat as the vanguard of the revolution indicates the non-dogmatic use of given ideologies by men such as Guevara and Fanon. For them, revolutionary symbols of self-transcendence are open to be construed in keeping with the needs of people in diverse situations. Fanon espouses the leadership of the people (peasantry) united to an intellectual elite that draws its power and inspiration from the people. This revolutionary vanguard is not only distinguished from the *lumpenproletariat,* but most especially from the native middle class. Fanon states: ". . . that African unity can only be achieved through the upward thrust of the people, and under the leadership of the people, that is to say, in defiance of the interests of the bourgeoisie."[15]

In another place he affirms that in underdeveloped countries the people together with the party and dedicated intellectuals "who are highly conscious and armed with revolutionary principles ought to bar the way to this useless and harmful middle class."[16] Fanon sees the native bourgeoisie as narcissistic, racist, and chauvinistic. Because their own selfish interests are uppermost, they will make the necessary compromises with the white rulers to maintain privileged black positions. These blacks have also adopted the prevalent racism of the society in that they shy away from their own blackness and look down on the poor Negro and Arab masses. They end up supporting France and its culture above national independence and the black heritage. A revolutionary of professional status, such as Fanon, could expect to be driven out of the political system by the native bourgeoisie, who fear to lose their own privileges. But these true revolutionaries can retreat to the people in the countryside, where they find support. Fanon's analysis of the native middle class is particularly trenchant, since he also enjoyed the advantages of that group before his total dedication to the revolution. But Fanon is less adequate in criticizing the weaknesses of the peasantry. Moreover, he was not able to formulate ways of keeping the native bourgeoisie from gaining control of the nation after the revolution.

Fanon's trust in the most oppressed groups of the populace reflects his Rousseau-like faith in the common people. He speaks in rapturous language about the awakening of the simple people to national consciousness and revolutionary endeavors. The poor tribes of the Algerian hills and plains take on a symbolic value of religious importance in that they point to transcendent dimensions of life and community:

> In undertaking this onward march, the people legislates, finds itself, and wills itself to sovereignty. In every corner that is thus awakened from colonial slumber, life is lived at an impossibly high temperature. There is a permanent outpouring in all the villages of spectacular generosity, of disarming kindness, and willingness, which can never be doubted, to die for the "cause." All this is evocative of a confraternity, a church, and a mystical body of belief at one and the same time.[17]

Of course, Fanon's practical purpose as a leading revolutionary intellectual was to rally and direct the masses toward the attainment of concrete goals in the struggle against the French. In this perspective, his eulogy of the people could be taken in part as a tract of encouragement toward solidarity in the revolutionary cause. Fanon was later to taste disappointment when the victorious masses fell back into some of the ways of the colonialists they had defeated. But Fanon's mystique of the people calls for still other explanations. The people as a creative repository for yet unrealized life possibilities constitutes for Fanon a symbol of religious transcendence within the revolutionary pursuit itself. "The People" is an evocative and motivating image that is at once immanent and transcendent. The people is the locus of friendship and support in his present strivings; but it is also the reality through which he transcends the stifling confines of racist self-hatred and strains toward new experiences of being: "I feel myself a soul as immense as the world, truly a soul as deep as the deepest of rivers, my chest has the power to expand without limit."[18] Thus the people becomes for him a mystical body through which he can be born again to unforeseen dimensions of life.

If the people were to attain the creative potential for self-transcendence of which they were capable, they had to be served and educated by authentic revolutionary intellectuals. Fanon talks about uplifting and developing the people. He is convinced that the masses are able of being taught anything, even the most complicated problems. The revolutionary leader, however, must really want to explain things to the people and not count as time lost his efforts at instruction. In Fanon's ideal understanding of the political situation, the party was to be an agency at the service of the people, not of the government. But the people's role in the revolutionary context is not only that of the learner; the folk is also a supreme teacher. Political leaders and intellectuals should be placed in close contact with the people to learn from their poverty and to observe the awakening and progress of their revolutionary consciousness.

Fanon opposes the cult of the hero/leader who would direct the people without allowing their full involvement in decision making and action. Fanon advocated an egalitarian and participational relationship between men in society. He rejected the hierarchies of master-slave and child-parent as inimical to the equality and mutuality of a democratic community. Rather, Fanon urges an interdependence of roles, a reciprocity of learning and teaching, serving and being served, in keeping with the talents and achievements of each person. Fanon's paradigm of the socialist society is one that maximizes democratic participation to the point of making it a religious experience. He speaks of the people meeting to discuss, propose, and plan as though such an event was a liturgical action. Such a rite is the opposite of traditional, folkloric rituals, in which the people were worked into a frenzy by shamans or rendered helpless before arbitrary gods. As the people progress into a new revolutionary consciousness of their own value and potencies, their liturgical action of democratic participation fosters a deeper solidarity in the group and empowers them by novel insights toward self-transcendent involvements. Fanon speaks of these gatherings as "liturgical acts": "They are privileged occasions given to a human being to listen and to speak. At each meeting, the brain increases its means of participation and the eye discovers a landscape more and more in keeping with human dignity."[19]

This revolutionary liturgy, as a true work of the people, manifests itself in a number of societal transformations. Participation in the struggle against foreign domination becomes a means of new self-transcendence in family relationships, as well as those between men and women. Families overcome long histories of feuding and animosities among themselves in the collective ecstasy of the revolutionary cause. These reconciliations involve such uplifting experiences as forgiveness, purification, and a growth of awareness. The relationship between father and son shifts from one of patriarchal authority and filial obedience to a mutual exchange between adults. The father, who in the past had banned his son's involvement in the rebellion, is converted to join his son in militant action. The son is no longer the compliant child, but he becomes the carrier of experiences of the awakened people. The father is thus able to see his son with new eyes, as a person of courage and superior values, who calls the father beyond the limitations of the old patriarchy to embrace the revolutionary national consciousness. A similar alteration occurs in the relations among the siblings toward the eldest brother, who in prerevolutionary times assumed a role like that of the patriarchal father. Brothers are now called upon to relate as equals in the rebel cadre; it has even happened that the younger brother would be the group leader. With the breaking of traditional role stereotypes, the elder brother could be approached in his true personhood. Thus the revolution became a means for inner transcendence toward a fellowship of equal and free persons.

During the national battle for liberation from colonialism, the mingling of fighting experiences and conjugal life strengthens the union between husband and wife, and raises it to a new plane. What had been a form of cohabitation for the sake of progeny and sexual satisfaction evolves into a wider and deeper union. As husband and wife incur dangers together and collaborate in the work of destroying oppression, the couple supersedes the customary roles imposed by traditional Algerian society. These roles tended to be hierarchical, functional, and somewhat impersonal. In the revolutionary situation, the couple is no longer shut in on itself, but participates in a movement that democratizes and ennobles the husband-wife relationship: "There is a simultaneous and effervescent emergence of the citizen, the patriot, and the modern spouse."[20]

Woman's place in society also undergoes a transformation. The revolution calls upon her to put aside the traditional veil for certain activities. Fanon describes the profound psychological implications of this act for the Algerian woman. The crisis that the unveiling provokes in her bodily sensibilities and mental attitudes forces her to develop a new self-understanding and comportment as a woman. She overcomes her past timidity and enhances her personhood through the liberating experiences of joining men as an equal in the national struggle. Women ceased to be mere components for the purposes of men; no longer were they silent before men, whose word in the past had been absolute law. Through her sufferings and contributions in the revolution, she radiated a new personality. As the old values and fears disappeared, "She literally forged a new place for herself by her sheer strength."[21] Fanon eloquently depicts woman's self-transcendence toward new levels of freedom and self-determination in community.

The above examples of transformations in personal and family relationships emphasize a kind of transcendence in revolutionary religiousness that Fanon referred to as "collective ecstasy." Ecstasy, a term traditionally associated with religious experience, means a standing away from the old self and the world as it was known under ordinary circumstances. Ecstasy was linked to mystic visions that removed the subject from this world to encounter heavenly wonders; it was reserved to a few saintly figures. Revolutionary ecstasy, on the contrary, does not withdraw a person from worldly concerns and engagements. But in the very midst of earthly strivings for a just and humane society, the revolutionary religious experience lifts many people to richer levels of existence and self-realization.

Fanon's morality is characterized by the intense friction that marks a Manichaean perspective. To overcome the total evil of colonialism, he urges hatred for the French settlers. The hatred of the master for the slave must be turned back against its source. Hate as a motivating cause for action is not inborn; it needs to be cultivated. He admonishes the revolutionaries not to be compromised by the friendly gestures of the settlers, who want only to mitigate the increasing danger to themselves of the revolutionary movement. Fanon notes that "hatred is disarmed by these psychological windfalls."[22] He seems to make no distinction between hating the evil and hating the evildoer. The rebel, in order to become free, must become the hatred that the oppressor embodies.

Yet, before we conclude that Fanon's morality is unswervingly dedicated to such limitless hatred, it is important to look at other, related dimensions of his ethical consciousness. For the evidence is conflicting. Some of the most compelling passages from his works call for a new humanism that will surpass that of the rapacious European colonists. He speaks of transcending the selfish individualism of the colonial period to attain a collective spirit of co-operation and sharing. He inveighs against the divisiveness of the settlers in contrast to the human unity being cultivated in the awakening people. The desire of Fanon the psychiatrist to discover and love man was not rejected by Fanon the revolutionary spokesman striving to build a more just society. The white-hot intensity of his final manifesto, *The Wretched of the Earth,* needs to be situated within the humane context of his life and efforts. For the same proponent of hatred in certain circumstances was also the reformer of mental institutions and the indefatigable physician of Arab refugee camps in Tunisia.

These mixed and conflicting data concerning the basic impulses of Fanon's morality make it difficult to conclude that his ethics is simply one of hate. Moreover, it should be remembered that Fanon had a practical and rhetorical purpose in his revolutionary writings. He wanted to motivate a fearful and self-depreciating people to forcefully combat a powerful and in many ways ruthless system. His rhetoric was geared to stir up an oppressed people for maximum resistance. This is not to infer that Fanon's rallying propaganda was hypocritically conceived; for he himself intensely hated the colonial regime. The objection can be justly raised, however, that those who make themselves into hating persons may not be the best candidates for the humanistic society envisioned on the victorious side of the revolution. But, given Fanon's Manichaean starting point, his morality of the revolutionary struggle for decolonization had almost of necessity to be one of direct reversal of the Manichaean hatred of the natives expressed by the settlers.

The direct expression of the ethic of hatred is the doctrine of violent revolution, for which Fanon has become a leading modern theoretician. He upholds violent revolution from the standpoint of practical politics as well as from the perspective of sociopsychological emancipation. From his early experiences of ruling elites in Martinique, he knew that those who wield oppressive power over others for the sake of material gain and feelings of power will cling tenaciously to their dominance. "Colonialism," he maintains, "is not a thinking machine nor a body endowed with reasoning faculties."[23] Appeals to rationality or sentiment make little headway in altering the control of powerful profiteers. The entrenched colonial system itself represents violence to the masses of the people. That this is largely a covert violence, which operates the economic and political patterns of the colony, does not lessen its violent character. Fanon speaks of this situation as violence in its natural state, which will yield only when confronted with greater violence. It should also be remembered that Fanon witnessed the open violence of the French, who killed millions of Moslems during the war. From an ethical point of view, Fanon's counterviolence can be understood as legitimate self-defense or as a necessary means to overthrow a tyrannical regime, with the purpose of establishing a more humane social order.

But, for Fanon, violence in the revolutionary battle is not only a practical measure, nor simply a political means to an end. It is also the key to personal and communal liberation on a psychological plane. To the native, who dreams of retaliating against his persecutor, violence contains in itself a freeing energy. It becomes a cleansing force by which the native is liberated from his inferiority and self-hatred. The use of force against the oppressor causes the native to overcome his fear and despair, while it also puts him on the road to a renewed self-respect. In a more positive vein, Fanon sees the native's violence as an act whereby he re-creates himself as a man. By curing what Sartre calls "the colonial neurosis" through participation in armed revolt, the native experiences a new wholeness and self-possession. Violence, furthermore, has a communal effect of unifying the people and instilling into them "the ideas of a common cause, of a national destiny, and of a collective history."[24] Colonialism is by its nature separatist; it keeps the tribes divided along the lines of ancient animosities so that they can be more readily manipulated for the settlers' advantage. Revolutionary violence, according to Fanon, fosters an all-inclusive form of national unification. Thus violence becomes a liberating therapy for the individual rebel as well as for the communal consciousness of the new nation aborning.

In the period of the revolutionary war, violence becomes an avenue for self-transcendence, because it leads to personal and communal wholeness, according to Fanon. In the colonial past of his people, he saw violence misdirected in self-destructive forms of religious frenzy. The native directed violence against himself and his fellow blacks. Or, influenced by the fatalism of God's will through traditional religions, the native resigned himself to his disintegrated destiny. Again, the Algerian was wont to release his pent-up violence in wild rituals and dances. These false ways of religious transcendence in a repressive colonial situation were encouraged both by tribal religious customs and also by the Christianity of the settlers. Fanon saw his role during the Algerian war as the prophetic spokesman who strove to reorient the native violence of the people against the colonial regime as the only way to true self-transcendence in a basically repressive environment.

But this doctrine of violence raises serious questions on both the ethical and the therapeutic levels. From a moral perspective, Fanon's advocacy of violence can be justified as an exercise of self-defense and liberation from a tyrannical colonial situation. It is beyond the scope of this inquiry to examine the extent of the oppression in Algerian society and other factors that would justify such a violent response. In the light of most ethical perspectives, Fanon's glorification of violence would be seen as reprehensible. But, again, his concentration on violence must be seen in the larger context of the revolutionary war for liberation. It is within that somewhat limited domain that violence takes on meaning for Fanon. His hope, even in the time of war, was for a more just society, in which violence would subside and men would treat each other with dignity and respect. It should not be forgotten that Fanon stood not only for violence but also for reconciliation. Simone de Beauvoir remarked at Fanon's own sense of repulsion from the horror of the killing in North Africa.

Fanon does not propose indiscriminate violence. He notes that many in the native middle classes are more inimical to the revolutionary cause than certain sons of the colonists, who sympathize with the revolution. Fanon himself was aided by French sympathizers with the Algerian cause. He received help from them both in his literary pursuits and in his revolutionary movements. Although he urged a discerning use of force, Fanon showed little esteem for the nonviolent stance on either practical or theoretical grounds. He tended to associate nonviolence with the native bourgeoisie, who seek to use it for self-serving ends. Fanon, whose morality is one of intense action, saw the nonviolent approach as too passive for achieving specific results. He does not appear to have gained an appreciation for the strength and effectiveness of nonviolent modes of resistance in other freedom struggles. But his desire for some kind of nonviolent resolution of conflict after the revolution reveals a person who ultimately wanted to transcend violence. He even believed that the violence exercised in the Algerian war would facilitate nonviolent revolutionary activities for liberation in other places.

As to the therapeutic value of violence, Fanon's own psychological research and clinical experience reveals contradictory evidence to his own claims. For he reports cases of mental disorders in persons on both sides of the conflict; these illnesses were in most instances linked to the exercise of violence. On the level of community, the healing potential of violence is also unclear. The dilemma might be expressed in this manner: how can a people resort to rapid, violent social change without endangering all the values in their heritage? On both individual and collective planes, violence is risky and ambiguous as to its therapeutic value. The necessary brutality of war can dehumanize a person and make him less able to live in peace with his neighbors after the violent experiences. Moreover, a society accustomed to the violence of guerrilla warfare can degenerate into a milieu in which life becomes cheap and expendable.

Despite these dangers, a significant therapeutic dimension can be admitted as a possibility for those who forcefully throw off a racist and exploitive system. For in the midst of the revolutionary struggle, violent resistance becomes a factor in the dialectic of human self-transcendence. By fighting for the cause of national liberation, the native undergoes the *metanoia* of rejecting with his mind and body a false self-image and a set of values imposed on him by the colonists. In his violent pursuit of freedom, he confronts death itself in both physical and spiritual ways. To die physically in the revolution is to defeat the death of the spirit, the death of self-hatred taught by the colonial regime. For the native comes to realize that ". . . we only become what we are by the radical and deep-seated refusal of that which others have made of us."[25] By violently renouncing the identity of himself that the oppressor has imposed on the native, a new freedom of mind and body is experienced. Such liberation can be seen as the positive side of the *metanoia* involved in violent resistance. It can be both therapeutic and religious in as much as it opens the native to transcendent dimensions of human existence that the colonial situation had rendered impossible.

The violent revolutionary struggle also contributes to a new sense of community: "The practice of violence binds them together as a whole . . . the group recognizes each other and the future nation is already indivisible. The armed struggle mobilizes the people . . . it throws them in one way and one direction."[26] The depth and permanence of this unification of community through violent conduct can rightly be questioned. But the experience of a new sense of community in the violent struggle is an important aspect of Fanon's religiousness. The traits of this community were already forming during the Algerian campaign itself. Its general lineaments were those of a socialist society, which would stress co-operation over competition, social needs over individual profit. A key element of this society would be the redistribution of wealth according to human needs. Fanon's travels through Europe and Third World countries convinced him that the fundamental question, beneath the duels of capitalism and socialism, was that of the redistribution of wealth. Fanon also called on the colonial nations of Europe for material reparations to nations such as Algeria as a measure of justice after many years of exploiting the land.

The reorganization of the economic and political structures of society, however, would call for a change of attitude on the part of all persons in the socialist community. The mentality of selfish individualism would have to change to one of communal responsibility. Fanon even speaks of this change in traditionally religious language when he condemns the narrow, self-seeking subjectivism inculcated by the colonial culture as "the atheist's method of salvation."[27] It is noteworthy that all the great religious traditions of the West stress community over individualism, communal trust and love over isolated, individual pursuits. Individual self-realization is also important to Fanon, who spent many years as a psychiatrist endeavoring to help individuals find an inner center of self-worth. The value of each individual, however, is intimately related to his place within community. Democratic participation of each individual in decision making and action within community becomes the way by which the revolutionary person attains self-fulfillment.

As a diplomat for the Algerian National Liberation Front, Fanon traveled widely in Africa. He became ever more conscious that other forms of chauvinistic narrowness, those of tribalism and nationalism, had become great obstacles to the enlargement of community into a fuller unity of Third World peoples. In the last year of his life, Fanon became an emissary for the unification of blacks to aid in the expulsion of the French from Algeria. He found that the chief drawbacks to this African unity were tribalism and the selfish interests of the native middle classes. Beyond the immediate goal of unifying his African brothers behind the Algerian cause, he envisioned the coming together into a novel community of universalism and equality all the nations of the Third World. Thus, toward the end of his neo-Manichaean stage, Fanon's experience of self-transcendence was enriched by symbols of a universal and equitable brotherhood.

His revolutionary involvements became the catalysts for an expanded sense of community as part of his religious experience.

The third phase of his life, that of Manichaean dualism resolved in the creation of a new socialist people, had already begun in the experiences of self-transcendence described above. On the levels of meaning, affection, and morality, Fanon's subjective motivating images were shaped by the events and immediate aspirations of his revolutionary engagements. Yet a discussion of Fanon's religiousness would be incomplete without considering the objective symbols of self-transcendence that constitute the visionary and eschatological dimension of his experience. This realm of ultimacy, toward which all the partial symbols point, can be summed up as the New Humanity (NH). Although Fanon can foresee and depict some characteristics of the NH, it remains an undetermined and open-ended symbol of ultimacy.

The NH for Fanon is a utopian image in the etymological sense of "no place," that is, the utopia cannot be circumscribed and delimited by human manipulation. Of course, man remains an active self-creator and fashioner of his own history. But none of these activities fully comprehend the NH; it is a futuristic symbol that points to a kind of existence not yet realized. Fanon indeed speaks of the actual revolution as the "oxygen which creates and shapes a new humanity."[28] Yet, all these partial realizations still fall short of the NH as an undefined, futuristic symbol that comes to the revolutionary as a source of power and as a gift. It is glimpsed in the empowering that he experiences from his gratuitous incorporation into the revolutionary people. For Fanon, the NH also performed the function of a criterion of judgment, as an ideal against which the revolutionary would have to measure each advance or regression in the pilgrimage of a revolutionary people. As a transcending ideal, the NH operated against the historical absolutizing of any given stage in the revolutionary advance. From this vantage point, the NH is immanent in history as a partially realized ideal, but it also transcends history as a projection that defies human reckoning.

As a probing psychiatrist in the Antilles and France, Fanon was already looking toward a new humanism, whose dimensions exceeded the world he knew: "In no fashion should I undertake to prepare the world that will come later. I belong irreducibly to my time."[29] For Fanon, the realizing of the transcendent is embodied in the NH. In this regard, the prophet of revolutionary violence is also a harbinger of hope. His religious experience becomes a call forward toward the ultimacy of the NH, which he wants to realize as much as possible in this world. It is in this outlook of active hope that he leaves his final earthly testament:

> For Europe, for ourselves, and for humanity, comrades, we must turn over a new leaf, we must work out new concepts, and try to set afoot a new man.[30]

Footnotes

1. Frantz Fanon, *Black Skin, White Masks* (New York: Grove Press, 1968), p. 192.
2. Frantz Fanon, *The Wretched of the Earth* (New York: Grove Press, 1968), p. 41.
3. *Black Skin,* p. 116.
4. *Wretched,* p. 42.
5. *Black Skin,* p. 63.
6. *Black Skin,* p. 197.
7. *Black Skin,* p. 198.
8. Frantz Fanon, *Toward the African Revolution* (New York: Grove Press, 1969), p. 23.
9. *Wretched,* p. 223.
10. *African Revolution,* p. 170.
11. *Black Skin,* p. 229.
12. Ibid.
13. *Black Skin,* p. 222.
14. Ibid.
15. *Wretched,* p. 164.
16. *Wretched,* p. 175.
17. *Wretched,* pp. 132–33.
18. *Black Skin,* p. 140.
19. *Wretched,* p. 195.
20. Frantz Fanon, *A Dying Colonialism* (New York: Grove Press, 1967), p. 114.
21. *Dying Colonialism,* p. 109; also *Wretched,* p. 202.
22. *Wretched,* p. 140.
23. *Wretched,* p. 61.
24. *Wretched,* p. 93.
25. *Wretched,* p. 17.
26. *Wretched,* p. 93.
27. *Wretched,* p. 101.
28. *Dying Colonialism,* p. 181.
29. *Black Skin,* p. 13.
30. *Wretched,* p. 316.

Bibliography

Fanon, Frantz. *A Dying Colonialism*. New York: Grove Press, 1967.
————. *The Wretched of the Earth*. New York: Grove Press, 1968.
————. *Black Skin, White Masks*. New York: Grove Press, 1968.
————. *Toward the African Revolution*. New York: Grove Press, 1969.
Caute, David. *Frantz Fanon*. New York: The Viking Press, 1970.
Geismar, Peter. *Fanon*. New York: Dial Press, 1971.

VIII - Reflections on Dissenting Spirituality

Up to this point in the study, a working model for the religious experience as intrinsic to the human experience has been used as an interpretative device for understanding the religiousness of six revolutionary figures. In this final chapter I would like to accomplish two interrelated tasks. The first, a more theoretical enterprise, will be to formulate a general theory of human religiousness that emanates from the concrete lives of the subjects of this inquiry. The second goal of these concluding remarks will be to delineate more specifically the traits of a revolutionary spirituality as derived from the previous investigation of the six personalities. In the latter discussion, a critical appraisal of the findings should permit a discerning appropriation of aspects of revolutionary spirituality into contemporary life styles. It should be noted again that the revolutionary mode of spirituality does not exhaust the possibilities for human religiousness. Dissenting spirituality is simply one important way of being religious in the present era.

The word "spirituality" is not understood in some esoteric sense of traditional or modern religious cults or rites. Rather, the realm of the human spirit defines what is truly characteristic of man in relation to other animal species. This is not a plea for a rigid discontinuity between men and animals; science continues to shed valuable light on the significant relationship of humans and their animal antecedents. But from a phenomenological point of view, it can be adequately argued that certain manifestations of the human species are particularly characteristic of itself. These dimensions of being human can be summarized under the term *creative freedom*. Man's ability to choose and act, individually or in contact with others, is at the heart of his ability to transcend himself and enhance life in community. Creative freedom presupposes a questioning mind, which, by identity and contrast, projects images and ideals for the sake of new realizations in personal and societal existence. It is, of course, clear from reflection on the lives of the six radical figures that this creative freedom is limited in many ways. The existential restrictions of death and human frailty combine with negative societal and cultural factors to hem in creative freedom. Even positive actions toward liberation are beset with the limitations of mistaken vision, poor planning, and ill-timed execution. Moreover, man as a finite freedom is confined by his responsibility for the rights and needs of other humans, whom he ought not manipulate indiscriminately for his own ends, however creative these may seem.

Despite these restricting determinants, man's peculiar spirit reveals itself in the mental questing, affective longing, and willed action that infuse creative freedom. I have located the primordial religious experience within this human élan to transcend the past and present for the sake of richer meaning and community. For revolutionaries, this basically spiritual drive is nuanced by specific concerns and commitments. Yet their radical dynamic is eminently a spirituality, that is, it is rooted in the basic human orientation toward wisdom and love. But the question persists as to how this human spirituality can be called religious.

To clarify this issue, it will help to think about the genesis of traditional religious language and institutions in human history. Religious language sets are symbol systems by which men, as finite but creative freedoms, have attempted to cope with fundamental problems of human meaning and existence. These language sets are the historically conditioned embodiments of the spiritual dynamism of the human species to integrate (make whole) in thought and action the dilemmas and paradoxes of life and death. Traditional religious symbol systems are ways of getting a holistic grasp on the meaning and direction of personal, societal, and cosmic history.

With the institutionalization of these language sets, the fundamental continuum between the spiritual élan of finite, creative man and this élan's historical religious embodiments has been obscured. Issues of divinity and mystery became a distinct and special preserve of traditional religious institutions, as crystallized in myth and ritual; or these boundary problems about human and cosmic wholeness became the domain of gurus, who by personal charisms linked to accepted religious language sets, showed ways toward self-transcendent integration. A result of this historical development has been the strong tendency to break the continuum between the human and the religious, to seek the latter principally within the narrower zone of myths and rituals rather than in the warp and woof of daily secular existence.

The lives and deeds of the six men in this study confirm the basically secular orientation of human spirituality. Their religiousness is secular, not because in certain cases it opposes institutional religions or because it fails to explicitly name God. Rather, the dissenting spirituality of these contemporary personalities is secular in the sense that it is an intrinsic dimension of human striving. Nor is it a dimension of the human in a compartmentalized way; religiousness pervades the whole of human existence in as much as the latter is understood as a quest for the integration of self, history, and cosmos. An explicit awareness and naming of deity is not the chief watershed between the religious and the human. While a traditional language set of religious terms and concrete ecclesiastical attachments may empower a particular revolutionary in his search for liberating and integrating self-transcendence, these conventionally religious factors are secondary phenomena that only partially symbolize the core thrust of human religiousness.

Moreover, the institutions and symbols of conventional religion are to be evaluated by the criterion of whether they contribute to the holistic task of personal self-transcendence toward freedom in community. The religions of the world, therefore, are valuable to the extent that they foster the deeper yearnings of human religiousness. By such a claim I take with utter seriousness the tenets of progressive Christian churchmen and ecclesiastical bodies to the effect that the purpose of the church is to serve the world and that the church must be subordinate to the kingdom of justice, peace, and freedom in the secular.

Revelational religions may critique the human religiousness that I am describing for a lack of grace, gift, or gratuity, which is implied in a divine dispensation to man. Secular spirituality is said to be Pelagian, steeped in prideful human efforts wthout recourse to trusting faith. Yet the criticism stemming from the gratuity of grace is itself a gratuitous allegation against human religiousness. Throughout this study, I have pointed out how even atheistic revolutionaries see the present struggle for liberation as well as the future community as gifts given them. Revolutionary insights, companions, and exploits are to a large extent unmerited graces, or gifts, for the radical individual.

Those standing in classically revelational religions also charge human spirituality with the *hybris* of a Promethean view of history. For secular revolutionaries, it is said, the end of history is within history and man alone creates this history. As a first reply to this objection I would affirm that a growing number of contemporary theologians contend that the goal of history is either in some sense within history or it is nowhere. I am here referring to such thinkers as Whitehead and Teilhard de Chardin, who reject dualistic and dichotomous views of reality for organic and this-worldly understandings of historical evolution. If Teilhard's omega point is in some fashion beyond history as we now know it, it is, nonetheless, in close continuity with the evolving universe. Briefly, the increasing focus of theology today on the values of the world and its transformational (rather than its cataclysmic or dispensable) destiny constitutes a historicizing of the religious perspective akin to that of secular revolutionaries.

Guevara and Fanon, for example, take a rather humble if optimistic stance toward the future of human development. Their objective symbols of self-transcendence, such as the New People or the New Humanity, remain relatively non-defined and open-ended. Thus these symbols both avoid idolatry and act as judgmental criteria for contemporary exploits. I wonder whether the *hybris* quotient of many traditional religionists is not greater than that of revolutionaries. For is it not a kind of Prometheanism to be so certain about God's promises concerning the end of history, as revealed in a specific tradition? Christian theologians, even of the more progressive type, hardly ever question their own faith-certainties on this matter.

The humanistic revolutionaries, moreover, manifest a kind of faith that is neither Pelagian nor Promethean. On a prereflective level their perilous life orientation shows a fundamental "leap of trust" in the worth of life and the potential for meaning and creativity in the world. This primordial faith cannot be substantiated by rational argument or by ideological commitment. On the secondary plane, of theoretical revolutionary doctrine, a form of faith or trusting hope is also in evidence. The revolutionary often must battle overwhelming odds that appear to make his vision unattainable. That the new consciousness and the new society will be realized is an enormous act of faith. On both levels, furthermore, this faith possesses dimensions of gift, or gratuity. The revolutionary's prereflective confidence in the order and worth of existence is largely given to him by his formative life experiences with family and friends. Ideological confidence and hope is also gratuitously offered to him from revolutionary movements in past history and in his own experience. He does not create the revolution out of his own heart and head. Rather, he responds to concrete circumstances that call to him out of the sufferings of the people.

As a prelude to considering the traits of dissenting spirituality, it is important to understand the dynamic structure in which these characteristics are manifested. In the lives of all six revolutionaries, religiousness is revealed in the midst of an intense dialectic. This movement of conflict and resolution can be conveniently described in the general categories of the Hegelian dialectic. The moment of thesis represents intense awareness of an involvement in the suffering and oppression of a given group. The antithesis is the revolutionary response to the condition of evil on the levels of ideology and action. The synthesis consists in various partial attainments of revolutionary goals, but the incompleteness and inadequacy of such realizations need to be stressed. The ultimate ideals that infuse the motivating ideology and affections of the revolutionary antithesis remain, even in the third phase of the dialectic, only relative achievements. From what has already been said about the open-ended dimension of ultimate symbols for revolutionaries, it is crucial to their spiritual dynamic that the synthesis be defined and limited and thus open to new enhancement. Total achievement of ideals would not only eliminate the healthy tension of striving and growth, but it would also mean a kind of idolatrous divinization of the status quo.

It may seem strange that a dialectical spirituality is being discussed in terms apparently external to the individual revolutionaries. A spirituality or mystique is ordinarily thought of as a highly personal network of motivations. This is also true of the revolutionary; his spiritual experience is of personal self-transcendence toward enhancement of freedom in community. But his inner dialectic is especially conjoined to concrete and communal causes outside the self. The external dialectic of the revolutionary struggle informs and shapes his inner identity and aspirations. In this sense the spiritual dialectic of the revolutionary stresses historical praxis. This powerful centering of self on the sociopolitical process will in certain ways entail a lessening of introspection and thus a diminishment of psychological insight into the self.

It is at this point that Freudian and other types of intrapsychic therapeutics would criticize a revolutionary spirituality. The psychiatrist wants the revolutionary to explore his motivations and anxieties in the light of earlier personal and familial conditioning. He might also want to reduce the revolutionary's ideals and involvements to misguided forms of psychological projections. So also would traditional religious spiritualities take to task a mystique that focused too exclusively on social commitments and this-worldly concerns. The religious guru would point out the revolutionary's deficiencies in meditational experience and his failure to recognize the mystic dimensions of reality. Such criticisms are in part valid; revolutionary spirituality should lay no claim to being the only way to personal self-transcendence.

Yet, on the credit side of dissenting spirituality, its political and social aspects offer indispensable correctives to the shortcomings of its critics. The personal and subjective emphasis of much contemporary psychology tends to withdraw a person from the struggle for social change. According to an assumption underlying this whole study, a narrow focus into personal introspection can stunt the human and spiritual development desired in both psychology and religion. To make the presupposition clearer, it can be stated boldly: the non-political person is only half alive. Although involvement in social and political causes can be a form of escape or of power seeking, it can also be the occasion for deeper self-discovery. Engagement in the struggles of social change became for each of the revolutionaries in this study a means of self-knowledge as well as a platform for political action.

The more-directly intrapsychic modes of self-transcendence, such as psychological therapy and religious meditation, tend to remove a person from the difficult but rewarding school of sociopolitical reality. The counselor's office is in many ways an artificial milieu where a client can gain some insight and strength. But such therapy usually limits itself to the resolution of personal or familial problems. The wider social and political dilemmas that may also be contributing to the patient's difficulties are often ignored or considered very secondary matters. The client is helped to fit again the given social structure rather than challenge and strive to change it.

While introspection through religious meditation or drug use can deepen self-perception and external awareness, these methods of self-transcendence also avoid coming to grips with the hard realities of social injustices and political power struggles. The otherworldly forms of conventional piety also anesthetize the believer into a condition of false well-being or of comfortably accepting the evils of the status quo. The dissenting spirituality of revolutionaries calls for a wider vision of the human predicament that moves beyond intra-psychic or interpersonal issues to confront matters of social organization and power that daily impinge on people's lives. Self-knowledge and social responsibility are not contradictory in any of the above modes of self-transcendence. But direct focus on societal commitment in dissenting spirituality provides a special richness of total reality as a locus for personal and communal growth.

Traits of Dissenting Spirituality

By a retrospective look at the religiousness of the six revolutionaries I will delineate some of the more important characteristics of their dialectical and dissenting spirituality. The three moments of the dialectic of self-transcendence toward freedom in community must be understood as a continuous and overlapping process. My conception of the dialectic of revolutionary spirituality is only an interpretative device for co-ordinating both content and method with the dynamic movement of life. Although the dialectic may also involve rather clear stages of self-transcendence, as in the life of Malcolm X, it should not be simplistically interpreted as a temporally defined process of thesis, antithesis, and synthesis. Rather, within the complex flow of a particular life, dialectical moments will cross and interrelate in subtle ways. It is not a matter of spiritual progress that can be measured on a graph. Yet I believe that a mere listing of the traits of a revolutionary spirituality, without attempting to place them in a discernible dynamic, would impoverish the whole presentation. It is precisely within the polarities and tensions of the dialectical context of a dissenting spirituality that its particular marks make sense.

The thesis moment of the dialectic of dissenting spirituality entails an awareness of and involvement in the suffering situation of a particular group. The key traits of this phase of the dialectic are understanding of and empathy with the oppressed people. These two characteristics of understanding and empathy, although distinguishable, are intimately linked. Understanding implies a theoretical and practical grasp of the reasons for the exploitive situation. Understanding also calls for a motivating vision or perspective about ways to bring about a more humane and just society. But this understanding does not derive solely from theories and abstractions. The intellectual grasp itself is significantly fostered by the revolutionary's immersion in personal and communal struggles and sufferings. From such total encounters, intellectual knowing is enlightened and deepened by affective feelings and emotional experience. The result is a kind of empathetic understanding that defies easy categorizing.

If we turn to the lives of revolutionaries, the qualities of understanding and empathy can be concretely studied and described. For Guevara, vision and total participation are intimately related. His ideology of moving a people from alienation to new levels of reconciliation through the revolutionary struggle depends at every stage on a suffering involvement with the lot of the oppressed. In his speeches, he repeatedly urges those who previously enjoyed the benefits of privileged status to accept the sacrifices of sharing the fate of the victims of exploitation.

Like Guevara, Fanon linked his revolutionary views of transcending the Manichaean structures of colonial society to a populist mystique of direct contacts with the most deprived peasant class. As a leading propagandist for a new cause, he lyrically exaggerated the virtues and abilities of the countryside native. But his insistence on sharing at first hand the perceptions and feelings of the oppressed was aimed at overcoming the dualistic vacuity of a revolutionary theory separated from suffering involvements. He notes that traditional relations between father and children, among siblings, and between men and women underwent profound changes toward increased self-dignity and democratization. But in these and other areas new modes of interrelationship came about as a result of concrete participation in the tasks and dangers of guerrilla resistance. Sharing the daily existence of the guerrilla bands became a school for self-transformation. Both Guevara and Fanon declare by their actions that a revolutionary ideology fails to be an agent for significant personal self-transcendence without bodily involvement with its concomitant risks. Fanon was badly wounded and narrowly escaped violent death, while Guevara was killed in the Bolivian campaign.

Empathetic understanding as a keynote of the first phase of a dissenting spiritual dialectic stands out in Martin King. King's motivating vision of interracial brotherhood beyond the hateful divisions of black and white demanded from him sacrificial sharing in the condition of deprived blacks. His vision itself became experiential and successfully adaptable only after personal hardships, threats, bombs, and clubs from Montgomery to Memphis. King himself notes that in his religious pilgrimage it was the real experience of fear and of suffering that allowed him to discern the relative values of previously learned theologies. His personal self-transcendence grew out of this-worldly strivings, civil rights campaigns, and actions against war and poverty. In and through these involvements he underwent the purification and preparation of self for recognizing and fostering transcendent possibilities in the racist society. He could say that he had been to the mountain not because he received a speculative revelation of brotherhood from its summit, but because he painfully climbed it.

Malcolm X provides an outstanding example of the trait of empathetic understanding that both gives insight into self and discloses the depth of sociostructural evil. Neither Guevara, Fanon, nor King experienced in his mind and flesh the dehumanization of Malcolm, the self-hating criminal hustler enslaved to degrading white values. His prison reflections revealed to him the destructive course that he and many other blacks were conditioned to follow. Despite their black racism, Elijah's Muslims offered him the tangible experience of a caring community of his own race. The shared life of this strict cult was the touchstone for his radical vision of new black self-understanding and fellowship. He had to feel in the fibers of his being the jealousy and bias of the Black Muslims before he could be open to a wider vision. His Mecca perspective resulted from immersion in the emotions, actions, and human meetings of the pilgrimage.

Although the revolutionary is familiar with theoretical analyses of past revolutionary thinkers, these ideologies constitute only a secondary context for his activity. Moreover, the theoretical conceptions themselves are to be judged by and accommodated to the lived experience of the given liberation movement in each place. The primacy of human experience and praxis is the motivating thesis for all six subjects of this inquiry in their construction and refashioning of revolutionary world views. Empathetic understanding that stems from this praxis is also the impelling thesis for the radical's inner *metanoia*. Berrigan once spoke of painting the map of his life's journey with his own blood. This graphic statement underlines the quality of passionate solidarity with the abused and downtrodden in their efforts toward liberation.

In the present time of increased consciousness of social evils, many individuals are assuming a critical and revolutionary-like position toward established institutions and values. But the starting point of many radical intellectuals and activists today often strays from the thesis situation of our revolutionary subjects. Their dissenting spirituality originates in empathetic understanding of the lot of the oppressed. It does not start from ivory-tower speculations or from popular but ephemeral actions devoid of co-suffering and personal risk. Of all the revolutionaries studied in these pages, Abbie Hoffman is the weakest in embracing the thesis of the dissenting mystique. While he does manifest personal risk in his empathetic understanding, the depth of shared suffering with the downtrodden is lacking. Without the dimension of an empathetic understanding involving suffering participation, the revolutionary élan does not penetrate to the core of the radical person. The revolutionary movement tends to become academic or dilettantish. From the perspective of religiousness, failure to appropriate the thesis of dissenting spirituality impedes the personal experience of self-transcendence. Religious self-transcendence, according to the subjects of this study, calls for a total involvement of the person that requires self-sacrifice and even physical suffering. Only thus does the thesis of empathetic understanding become a point of departure for the dialectic of dissenting spirituality.

The empathetic understanding that characterizes the first moment in the dialectic of revolutionary spirituality opens the latter to its antithesis. Here antithesis is used in a somewhat different sense from what would normally be expected in a threefold dialectic. The movement of revolutionary action is not an antithesis to empathetic understanding, but rather to the structures and values of the oppression that the empathetic understanding has disclosed. The second movement of the dialectic of dissenting spirituality, therefore, opposes those forces in society that are understood to impede self-transcendence toward freedom in community. This antithesis, however, has both a negative and a positive pole. Revolutionary action is by definition a movement against certain institutions, persons, ideas, and values. It is a no-saying and a no-doing; more than that, revolutionary action is bent on actively overthrowing either whole regimes or at least dominant structures and attitudes within a society. Yet this negatively antithetical dimension of revolutionary practice is complemented by a positive pole of reconstruction or reconciliation. Revolutionary action is not nihilistic. It is, rather, an activity of reaction for the sake of positive attainments. Although dissenting spirituality stresses the movement of negation, it is never far from an assenting mystique concerning new possibilities. These positive aspects are only partially achieved in the third movement of synthesis, which itself opens to transcendent symbols. In the following section, I want to lift up from the lives of revolutionaries traits that mark both the negative and the positive dimensions of the antithesis of revolutionary activity.

Dissenting spirituality is characterized by strong opposition against institutions, forces, and attitudes that are viewed as destructive of man and community. This negative drive of the revolutionary is aimed against inner enemies of the psyche as well as external powers. Fanon the psychiatrist waged war against the demeaning self-hatred of Antilleans and Algerians who embraced the colonialist value system. His rage against a culture that prevented black self-acceptance intensified as he grew to realize that the intrapsychic enemies of the natives could not be vanquished without a negation of the whole colonial system. It was not enough to cultivate the virtues of negritude within the matrix of French domination. The antithetical thrust of his revolutionary action focused on thoroughly rooting out and surpassing the colonial matrix.

A similar negative drive is borne out in quite different ways in Hoffman's Yippie revolution. By exaggeration, ridicule, confusion, and irrational gestures, the prophetic jester attempts to exorcise the demons of Pig Nation that infest minds and hearts. Hoffman, more than Fanon, is convinced that revolutionary negation has to be directed primarily at the false consciousness in individuals. Their heads have to be changed before the social and political revolution can be successful. Hoffman's emphasis on attacking personal consciousness is partly attributable to a very different circumstance, a technologically advanced nation, where the tactics of Guevara and Fanon would be doomed.

Hoffman's psychic revolution is also conditioned by his own ideals of anarchistic individualism. But even Hoffman's attacks on individual consciousness are fashioned to stimulate a political and cultural revolution in the wider society.

Berrigan's negative activity is contained in his prophetic resistance to death forces in individuals and in the nation. Although the former is muted in comparison to the latter, he writes against the interior personal decay of servile conformity to a killing system. But his radical actions are mainly public no-sayings through the published word and dramatic actions such as draft-file burning. Yet the negative dimension in Berrigan, as with the other revolutionaries, involves an important element of self-suffering involvement. His prophetic no is not simply a denial of death-infested ideologies or a detached attack on other persons. His external dramatics of resistance demand that he sense the pain of struggle in his own body. By feeling in his flesh the weight and depth of his negations, these very denials are saved from being facile rhetoric or nihilistic exploits. The self-suffering of no-saying sensitizes his spirit to the burden of being prophetic, and it frees him from the bitterness and resentment that often accompany negation. Since he is not blighted by these effects of negativity, he becomes freer to experience in himself the freedom and hope that constitute the other aspect of the antithesis in revolutionary spirituality.

Malcolm X presents a striking example of the negative factor in the antithesis phase of dissenting religiousness. He was ever a man on the attack against opponents. In his hustler days, he rejected his blackness, which he saw as an enemy of private gain and power. In his Black Muslim conversion, he turned against both the degrading features of his past and the evil white man, who imposed much of that degradation on him. Yet these two phases of negation in Malcolm's life reveal a significant difference. The denial of the earliest period was mainly for egocentric purposes, whereas the negations of the Muslim preacher have an altruistic orientation. He is bent on emancipating his black brothers and sisters from the induced self-hatred of a racist society. His condemnations of white America, albeit exaggerated in the language of Elijah Muhammad, emanate from a more selfless Malcolm, who was discovering a sense of mission to liberate his people.

After his Mecca experience, Malcolm continues to embody the unflinching antithesis to racism. By this time his perspective has broadened and become more discerning, but the intensity of his war on institutional and attitudinal racism has not abated. This third period of his life, moreover, manifests not only the unselfish aspects of his denials and confrontations; it also portrays his increased self-suffering in the midst of negations. He experiences the hurt of profound disillusionment with Elijah's group. He and his family become vulnerable in stark new ways from both blacks and whites; his home and life are in constant jeopardy. Like Berrigan, he comes to know in his own body the risks and sufferings of the revolutionary antithesis. As he pays the mounting costs of his dissenting stance, Malcolm grows in inner freedom and self-identity. It is finally the man who embraced the self-suffering of the last year of his embattled life that has become the energizing symbol for others who would follow the way of dissenting spirituality.

For persons who desire to incorporate more consciously into their lives the negative stance of the antithesis, the decade of the sixties was a privileged time. This was especially true in America, where an acute consciousness of systematic and sanctioned evils came to the fore. Many Americans lost their sense of innocence about benevolent national intentions abroad and at home. The gruesome militarism of the Indo-China war occasioned a sharp questioning of economic and diplomatic negotiations in the spirit of the cold war. Many of these ventures were seen to be motivated by selfish interests to extend our political power and maximize economic profit at the expense of less fortunate peoples. On the domestic scene, racism, poverty, and pollution called into question the meaning and purpose of American institutions and values. When the evils of greed and injustice are uncovered in all their starkness, the dynamic of no-saying intensifies in a society, especially among the young, who perceive with fresh clarity the hypocritical rift between hereditary ideals and actual practice. There is good reason to believe that the disenchantment with and critique of the American Way will continue in the decade ahead.

Certain aspects of the negative mystique embodied in the four figures just reviewed serve as guideposts for those whom religiousness inclines toward dissenting spirituality. First, their no-saying and doing is not paralyzed or suppressed by the immensity of the evil around them. These men are not reduced to the impotent stance of self-centered pique and resentment. From their empathetic understanding of shared life with the oppressed, they derive a staying power to resist against overwhelming odds. Secondly, the negations of these radicals are fundamentally altruistic. The struggle against various tyrannies and injustices is consistently oriented toward the liberation of other persons and communities. This is not to deny a portion of egoism and self-serving in all these personalities. But the principal direction of their no-saying words and deeds is ultimately altruistic. This other-directed dynamic of their negativities is confirmed in a sense by their willingness to risk their own material and personal security for the sake of the revolutionary cause.

The negative phase of antithesis in revolutionary spirituality necessarily implies violent or nonviolent means of opposition. In our study, Guevara and Fanon explicitly choose the violent route of negations, while Berrigan and King consciously champion nonviolent approaches in fighting evils. Malcolm X threatens violence, but actually resorts to active nonviolence in his intense battle against racism. The style of Abbie Hoffman, with its jester qualities and anarchistic sensibilities, focuses on psychic rather than physical violence to achieve his ends. Fanon comes closest to making violence an end in itself. When his words emphasize such a view, they militate against growth in religious experience. A glorification of violence for purposes of inner liberation is highly dubious. Fanon's own clinical work with the mentally disturbed indicated that many became ill by exercising violence. Done for itself, violence is not a catalyst for self-transcendence toward freedom in community, but rather it becomes a dehumanizing force for both the individual and the society that so wields power.

Yet, even in Fanon, violence is mainly set into a context of means for a more humane, less violent civilization. The employment of armed force for beneficial purposes implies, of course, the grave peril of vitiating the intended good by the very means used. Yet the covert violence of degrading and tyrannical regimes may be judged to be more dehumanizing than resort to revolutionary violence. This was certainly the evaluation of Guevara in certain Latin American situations. Although the use of violent force by Guevara in concrete instances was reprehensible by humane standards, the broad intentionality of his military operations must be placed in the context of combating an oppressively violent status quo. For Malcolm X, the threat of black violence in America was principally a defense measure against the personal and institutional violence of a racist land. Malcolm does not advocate the gun for itself or for aggressive domination of others. He does not actively seek to harm others, but he warns that great harm will come to the society if racism is not challenged. In the last year of his life, even these admonitions are set in a framework of bringing about the widest possible brotherhood among all races, a fellowship that would diminish resort to violence. Within the perspective of proportionately chosen means to liberate people from oppression, the violent negativities of the revolutionary antithesis are not intrinsically opposed to authentic religious self-transcendence.

Berrigan and King choose modes of negative action that are nonviolent for reasons both of principle and of effectiveness in a given milieu. These men sympathize with the goals of the violent revolutionaries and understand the unjust situations that impel them to violence. But King and Berrigan make a radically different choice of means with which to do battle. The chief principle prompting nonviolent direct action is the conviction that the revolutionary end, a more humane selfhood and community must already infuse and inform the means of struggle. They hold that violence generally breeds violence; actions toward a better society should reveal the humaneness of the envisioned society. Moreover, nonviolent resistance presupposes an optimistic view of human nature, namely, that the unjust opponent is good enough to acquiesce to truth when he experiences men suffering without violence to reveal the rightness of certain demands. Aside from the question of principles, it is very difficult to determine how much the nonviolence of King and Berrigan was dictated by the desire for practical results in the United States. King, far more than Berrigan, openly advocates nonviolent strategies for pragmatic ends. Finally, Christian and Gandhian tenets have an important influence on the nonviolent positions of both men.

The antithesis of the dialectic of revolutionary religiousness eventually confronts the radical reformer with a choice of violent or nonviolent negation. No easy formula for condemning violence in every instance will satisfy. But, since violence in itself is not a freeing action for individuals or groups and since it can engender a more vicious social order than the one attacked, it can be a factor in religious self-transcendence only as a last resort. The corrupting possibilities of violent negation are so great that the tactics of nonviolence are certainly preferable. For many individuals, conscience will allow no other recourse than nonviolent opposition. In terms of advancement in the religious experience of individuals and communities, nonviolence offers a vastly superior way.

But the way of Berrigan and King requires a fundamental alteration of sensibilities, an education away from the now dominant modes of human response between nations, races, and classes. At this stage in man's evolution, his individual and group exchanges with his fellows are still largely based on the need to dominate and coerce by more or less violent means. His inner fears and insecurities cause him to mistrust others and force them to serve his political will or his desire for economic gain. The witness of men such as King and Berrigan is a hopeful sign that the future progress of the human race may someday turn in the direction of nonviolence. A look at the present strife in the world may make such a prediction appear extremely utopian. But there is reason to believe that in an age of unprecedented potentials for mass destruction coupled with undreamed-of possibilities for co-operation in a technological civilization, new styles of human interaction will develop. This judgment calls for a positive long view of history in which the revolutionary antithesis of negation will not cease, but rather be transformed into nonviolent processes. In that future day, the religious experience of mankind will reach new heights of self-transcending freedom.

The dialectic of dissenting spirituality achieves partial synthesis within the revolutionary himself and also in the liberated community. The negations of the antithesis occasion positive breakthroughs to new levels of hopeful freedom in a broadened community. Hoffman's Yippie conduct of confrontation with dehumanizing conventions fosters in him a new sense of self-liberation. He feels unbound from the compulsions of Pig Nation, which rule the lives of most Americans. Of course, Hoffman gives an exaggerated and at times distorted picture of national mores; moreover, he fails to recognize the limitations of his own newly found freedom. But it is a mistake to read Hoffman for a balanced and modest appraisal of either American unfreedom or of Yippie liberation. It is enough to observe in this man a novel attainment of inner emancipation, of an enhanced and integrated self-possession. Although Hoffman's anarchist emphasis centers on self-liberation, he discovers and creates ways of becoming a participant in diverse communities. He opposes the parochialism of both Left and Right as he attempts to assimilate the feelings and attitudes of diverse social groups. For all their shortcomings, Hoffman's partial realizations of enhanced freedom in a wider community are intrinsic to his religious experience, that dynamic openness to transcendent life possibilities.

For Martin King the struggle against racial discrimination culminated in new experiences of freedom within himself. He felt a greater power of self-determination and interior liberty in his ability to rally effectively his own people against the enslaving milieu of white America. Each concrete achievement in the civil rights campaign was understood as another milestone of freedom. These partial syntheses of his dissenting mystique were themselves the results of freedom rides and freedom marches. Freedom for King meant responsibility for self and for others. The slave mentality erased the sense of a self capable of significant response to persons and situations. The slave was a possession to whom and for whom things were done; he was kept from becoming a responding self, a person of self-determination.

But the moment of synthesis in King's inner sense of liberation was increasingly linked to an outward thrust for communal freedom. As his charismatic leadership spread across nation and world, his understanding of social responsibility grew. His mission of liberation from racism was carried north as well as south; to whites, not only blacks. The goal of a freer brotherhood eventually transcended national boundaries to embrace the "world house." His concerns went beyond black issues to questions of international wars and poverty. It would be truer to say that he saw these wider problems as closely associated with racism and its perpetuation. Thus a trait of King's religious self-transcendence at its peak moments of synthesis was a growing sense of freedom in an ever-broadening community.

Malcolm X exhibited a similar characteristic of inner liberation as a part of his revolutionary struggle to overcome racial self-hatred in himself and among blacks. The points of synthesis in his dissenting spirituality were marked by new apprehensions of freedom. In his prison conversion to the Black Muslims, he referred ecstatically to his sense of liberation from the "niggerness" that lay like an unliftable pall over his previous life. He could finally accept his blackness and rejoice in it. But this inner freedom was intimately connected with the experience of community. Muhammad's Muslims provided the milieu of fellowship and concern in which his interior freedom could flourish. From his own emancipation experience, he became the preacher of liberation to fellow blacks still caught in the isolating bondage of slave conditioning in American society. After the Mecca pilgrimage, he attained the highest synthesis of liberation. He was then freed not only of his previous self-depreciation, but also from the narrowing confines of the Black Muslims' ideology of black superiority over white devils. Again, this final liberation was closely linked to the discovery of a wider community that transcended race, class, and nation. This sense of participating in and being strengthened by the wider human community conducted Malcolm to his most influential stage as a spokesman for black emancipation.

Guevara and Fanon reveal similar traits in their moments of synthesis. The Latin American guerrilla learned through the school of revolutionary action to emancipate himself from the values of a culture that he saw to be oppressively selfish and materialistic. He was able to gain the allegiance of soldiers, workers, and intellectuals, because he expressed in his person a freedom from physical fear and from the mental attitudes that long dominated the life of South America. Fanon, too, experienced in the Algerian battle for independence a heightened realization of his value as a black in contrast to the unfreedoms that pressed on his soul in both Martinique and France. Yet, for both Guevara and Fanon, these freedoms *from* became freedoms *for* new human alternatives in and through the empowering experience of community. Guevara's cadre and Fanon's *maquis* were the social matrices for the partial synthesis of freedom in the dialectic of their religiousness.

These social radicals sought to expand their revolutionary communities for the pragmatic purposes of victories over opposing forces. Guevara strove to consolidate leftist movements against the regimes of capitalist-ruled countries in the southern hemisphere. Fanon traveled through North Africa to rally support for the Algerian struggle against the French colonizers. The expansion of revolutionary peoples, therefore, had a clear goal of practical solidarity for the liberation battle at hand. Yet, for both Guevara and Fanon, the extension of revolutionary comradeship was not only motivated for pragmatic reasons of political power, but it was also aimed at forming a new community in which human potentials could be liberated. Fanon desired that the Algerian revolutionaries might become the vanguard of a civilization in which human freedoms could reach new levels of attainment. His vision of a New Humanity transcended the narrow sense of community that European nations had developed. Guevara's New People was the envisioning of a community whose socialist consciousness would cultivate the humanization of persons in ways never attained in societies oriented toward the monopoly of an elite class.

The traits of freedom within the individual and in societal relations is intricately joined to the experience of community in the partial synthesis of the dissenting dialectic of spirituality. The path of revolutionary religiousness, therefore, constitutes a summons to inner liberation of the person from the anxieties and fears that impeded his human growth. Yet the same radical road can itself defeat man's inner emancipation if it fills him with arrogant ideologies and unremitting hatred of opponents. These dangers are very real, especially for revolutionaries bent on direct violence; the revolution may represent a new bondage. Such destructive tendencies can be re-enforced if the radical cadre itself becomes a center of hatred and resentment. It is admittedly no easy task to maintain in the revolutionary community an attitude of clear-sighted opposition to social evils in a society, and well-planned actions to correct these wrongs, while at the same time not falling prey to self-destructive hatred and viciousness toward opponents. The revolutionaries in this study and their radical communities only partially master this delicate balance between uncompromising resistance to oppression and concern for the oppressor as a person and as a potential member of the wider community to be achieved. Yet, without action inspired by such an outlook, revolutionary spirituality becomes a euphemism for further enslavement of man, rather than his liberation.

Moments of synthesis in dissenting spirituality, as we have seen, relate growth in inner freedom and strivings for external liberation with an expanded sense of community. Yet this wider fellowship of mankind becomes in a technological civilization a most difficult achievement. Certain advances of technology have wonderful possibilities for widening the sense of human brotherhood; communication, transport, production are a few examples of areas that in an age of electronics and mechanization have vast potential for lifting men out of their alienating and hostile divisions. But the development of technology has also tended to intensify individualism as well as international animosities. With the development of great urban cultures, a spirit of individualism has flourished.

Anonymity and fragmentation have also characterized the history of modern technology. The latter's close connection to capitalism constitutes still another factor in movement away from a more organic and communal grasp of the human condition. Capitalism's principal emphasis on maximizing private gain orients people into intensely individualistic pursuits. Technology has also helped to engender an acute consciousness of and deep resentment about maldistribution of human resources and wealth. The political regimes judged to be responsible for individualistic imbalances and exploitation of the less favored masses are increasingly under attack. The dominant scenario around us, therefore, is one of a technological world threatened by the twin enemies of a broader human community: personal individualism and national hostilities. This scene of atomization and animosity is further complicated by the hatreds and fears that divide classes, races, religions, and political groups within and among nations.

In view of these destructive realities in contemporary society, the universalist spirit of the highest moments of synthesis in revolutionary spirituality take on special importance. All the figures in this study underscore the significance of complementing the revolutionary antithesis of negation and resistance with a vision of and feeling for a more universal brotherhood among peoples. Since the revolutionary posture itself focuses strongly on elements of antithesis, a constant peril exists of vitiating the possibilities for the synthesis of a more universal community. Yet, to abandon the antithesis is to abdicate responsibility for the necessary struggle. Moreover, without commitment to the tasks of antithesis, the causes of the old divisions among men cannot be overcome to make way for a fuller community. Yet, the empowering dream of universal brotherhood is reflected in the high points of dissenting spirituality. This vision acts as a maturing lure that gives meaning and purpose to the struggle against forces of alienation and exploitation.

The traits of freedom and community that mark the third phase of the dialectic of revolutionary spirituality portray an optimistic hope for man's historical future. It is precisely on this issue of historical hope that a number of contemporary Christian theologians put forth their main critique of the revolutionary mystique as manifested by radical figures dissociated from Christian or other traditional religions. Rubem Alves sums up this criticism of unbelieving revolutionaries in a particularly lucid manner. Alves distinguishes between a humanistic messianism and a messianic humanism.[1] The messianic hope of the mere humanist, argues Alves, claims that the task of human liberation will be realized by the powers of man alone. In contrast, the messianic humanist (i.e., the Christian radical) through his faith in God sees the future humanization of man chiefly as a gift. Alves maintains that the revolutionary hope of the humanist tends to degenerate into either romantic optimism that abandons historical realism or into a historical realism that sacrifices hope to cynicism and despair. Again, in contrast, Alves argues that: "It [messianic humanism] remains realistic without despair and hopeful without being romantic."[2]

The whole tenor of this study of the religious experience of revolutionaries contests the Alves thesis and its various orchestrations in the writings of other well-known theologians who in recent years have addressed the topic of religion and revolution. These men have made outstanding contributions to our understanding of political theology. But I find that the dragon of Christian superiority has yet to be slain in their works. Their faith seems to compel them to argue that ultimately the revolutionary believer and especially the Christian will be motivated by a theoretically and practically better form of hope. Yet a phenomenological and inductive investigation of concrete revolutionary persons urges us to be more modest in our apologetic comparisons of humanistic and Christian hope. It is simply not true to say of humanistic revolutionaries such as Guevara and Fanon that their historical hope was reduced to cynicism and despair. On the contrary, their hope for a New People and a New Humanity is as sober and confident as that of a Berrigan or a King. Nor can we conclude that the revolutionary humanist takes flight in naive futuristic romanticism abstracted from history. For all of Hoffman's theatrical escapades, a sense of Pig Nation's history remains, both as to its antecedent influences and its future prospects. Thus a closer inspection of individual revolutionaries does not bear out the Alves critique; theological theory can and should be tested by the lives and works of the men to whom it is intended to apply.

Moreover, the historical hope of revolutionaries, whether humanist-Marxist or traditionally religious in motivation, cannot be neatly distinguished according to a Pelagian/non-Pelagian criterion. As I have pointed out above, the future of history has an element of gift for both types of revolutionary. It might be argued that confidence in a personal God who opens and guides the way of the future is a firm basis for historical hope. Yet I hold that the humanistic revolutionary's open-ended symbols, such as the New People or the New Humanity, perform the same functions for strengthening historical hope as the directly theistic images. Humanistic ideals also act as gratuitous sources of power and value for the revolutionary; these images stand in

judgment on present attainments and to an important extent
they are beyond human manipulation. It is time that we stopped
trying to show how the Christian's revolutionary hope for the
future is superior to that of humanists. Surely Christian or Islamic hope will reflect a different motivating dynamism and
different historical nuances than humanistic trust. But differences do not necessitate the mutual rejection of one kind of
hope in order to follow the other. What matters, rather, is that
radical social reformers of whatever inspirational persuasion
accomplish the works of justice, freedom, and peace. It is ultimately by these concrete achievements that their theories will be
judged.

The general direction of this book lends itself to drawing a few
tentative conclusions. If the guideline model used in this study
is an adequate working theory for coping with the religious experience, the latter is to be found primarily in a person's total
secular life orientation. Religiousness is intrinsic to human becoming in as much as the latter is motivated by open-ended
symbols of self-transcendence toward freedom in community.
This perspective helps to integrate the worldly and the religious
dimensions into a unified secular orientation open to the mystery
of reality and the enhancement of present and future values.
Only in a secondary sense is the religious experience to be
identified with adherence to doctrines, rituals, institutions, or
the ways of particular gurus. These traditionally religious matrices of spirituality can continue to be significant empowering
milieus for many. Moreover, churchly ecumenism today can also
realize important unities among divided ecclesiastical bodies and
world religions. But in the light of this study, I would conclude
that this secondary ecumenism of traditional religious groups
loses its main purpose if it is not directed toward the primary
task of promoting the deepest reaches of the religious experience
intrinsic to being human.

When we look at the lives of particular revolutionaries through
the lens of the working model of religiousness, traditional demarcations for defining the religious sphere give way to a more

humanistic understanding. At this stage of our inquiry, we can restate that Che Guevara is as religious as Dan Berrigan, although under different modalities of expression. Another premise in this judgment is that the Christian religious language of a Martin King, although very important for him personally as a historical source of inspirational images, becomes a code system for talking about deeper human motivating symbols. Neither just distribution of goods nor political power is ultimately crucial for Guevara; nor are traditional concepts of church or God what finally matter in the intentionality of Berrigan's strivings. In and through these secondary symbols, the dynamic of self-transcendence in such men is chiefly directed by the this-worldly, open-ended symbolism of a freer human consciousness in a new human community.

Finally, the orientation of this study invites us to trace out some implications for formulating a dissenting mystique for our time. A number of writers have criticized the clericalist, dualistic, and legalistic hue of much classical and modern Christian spirituality. Yet a truly worldly and communal kind of dissenting spirituality remains to be developed. I have endeavored to draw out of the particular lives of revolutionaries the main traits of a dialectical understanding of the religious experience. I do not claim that dissenting religiousness, as witnessed in the lives of these six men, is the only authentic way of being religious. But this dialectical mode of spirituality intrinsic to the human experience goes beyond the customary confines of what is considered religious. Such religiousness has been too long neglected by both religious scholars and institutions. Moreover, in the present period of sociopolitical upheaval, dissenting spirituality takes on a special significance. It is a way of being religious, of personal and communal self-transcendence, for those involved in the struggles for human freedom and reconciliation.

Footnotes

1. Rubem A. Alves, *A Theology of Human Hope* (Washington: Corpus Books, 1969), pp. 185–87, 98–99.
2. Ibid., p. 100.